Dr. Anne
Marie
Evers ~

HIKE OF LIFE ADVENTURE

Namasté
precious soul

♡ Joréé

my hope is
that when you read
this book your heart is
touched and you create
for yourself a new
beginning in some
way!

HIKE OF LIFE ADVENTURE

Lorill B. Estar

JANUS PUBLISHING COMPANY
London, England

First Published in Great Britain 2005 By
Janus Publishing Company Ltd,
105-107 Gloucester Place
London W1U 6BY

www.januspublishing.co.uk

"In Roman mythology Janus is the God of all doors,
gates and entrances – and hence of all beginnings."

British Library Cataloguing-in-Publication Data
A catalogue record for this book
is available from the British Library

ISBN 1 85756 573 8

Cover Design Nathan Cording

Printed and bound in Great Britain

Disclaimer

The author of this book does not, either directly or indirectly, dispense medical advice or prescribe the use of any technique as a form of treatment for physical, emotional, or medical problems without the advice of a physician.

The intent of the author is only to offer information of a general nature to help the reader in their quest for inner peace.

In the event that the reader uses any of the information in this book, that is your right, but the author and the publisher assume no responsibility for your actions.

"The trail is wide, the way is safe...
you are not alone on the journey of life"

To Grace Eleanor Mackinder,
for the gift of life, and every expression
of Spirit in my experience.
Without you I would not be who I am.

Contents

Preface

I take a step of vulnerability to share with you aspects of my process, my hike of my life adventure, in the hope that you will: acknowledge that you are not alone; embrace and accept the truth of your humanity; entertain the notion and the importance of making inner connections rather than outer corrections; and accept that life is an ongoing series of experiences.

As we evolve as individuals, we learn from our experiences and we make new and different choices to effect life-giving changes when we desire to create different results.

What I know for myself is that I could not possibly experience peace in my external world until I had experienced peace in my internal world. I must admit though that for years I had the unrealistic expectation that others ought to change and then I'd be happy and at peace. My dissatisfaction with my life made me angry and the anger energy, used constructively, propelled me to change how I thought, to create the changes I desired. Oh, I spent a couple of decades endeavouring to change the external so I would feel differently internally. I changed jobs, relationships, lost weight, tried new hairstyles to change my physical appearance, changed where I lived, vacation destinations, the cars I drove, activities, habits, and still there was an ache within that none of the externals would dissipate. It wasn't until I began to diligently and consistently change the thoughts I chose to think that my life began an incremental life-giving transformation and the inner ache dissolved and I experienced ever-increasing degrees of freedom from self-destructive behaviours, addictions, and self-condemnation.

In this text there are eight nature photographs. Six are utilised to creatively introduce you to perceptions and techniques that may inspire you to feel, deal, heal your past by revealing to yourself the microscopic truth of life experience. Nature is so very nurturing, because it does not judge. I hope you feel the unconditional loving energy of nature through these photographs, taken during my two-year pilgrimage around the world. In the hustle and bustle of a busy urban life you may not have the opportunity to make this basic sustaining connection to life, expressing in and through nature.

I have included some of the inspiration in the form of poems that evolved through my process. I share quotes from authors, ideas from courses, lyrics from songs, dialogue from a couple of movies, and some stories about people I met along the way that may provide you with support.

In my own life, I experienced the self-destructive consequences of keeping my past a secret and the life-giving consequences of revealing and healing. I highly recommend the latter rather than the former.

I invite you to make the hike of life adventure. Give yourself permission to be eclectic. What do I mean by eclectic? Give yourself permission to take and incorporate into the hike of life adventure that which resonates with you, to realise the results you desire. Only you know what is best for you!

There are numerous ideas, perceptions, tools, and techniques to experience. The contents of this book are excerpts from nearly two decades of personal self-study development, and it would more than likely be overwhelming if you tried all the ideas at the same time.

Be gentle with yourself and proceed in a way of ease, in a way that is most compatible with yourself, and enjoy the journey!

Welcome to the lush field of life – a new beginning. You are a precious creation of the divine, just like the flower in the foreground of this photograph. You are unique, beautiful, innocent, growing in a limitless field of your life experiences.

Lush Field of Life – Limitless Paths

Imagination exercise

I invite you to relax, put your feet flat on the floor, read the meditation slowly and thoroughly a few times, then close your eyes to outer distraction and open yourself to this creative meditation visualization process.

Have you ever experienced your logical rational mind objecting when you attempt new things? Does it say something like: "Oh, this is silly" or "This isn't going to work" or "What a load of bull?" In any case, let's silently dialogue with that part of you that will think of all the excuses why you should not do this imagination exercise. Give this aspect of yourself a name: _____. "Okay _____, I hear you and although you have interesting things for me to consider, I choose to open to this new experience. I want to learn and grow in understanding and awareness of myself and others. I do not need you at present, so please take a rest and relax. Thank you!"

Take a couple of long, slow, deep breaths. With each conscious breath, you become calm, and you are willing and open to this simple safe exercise. I invite you to relax and take a good long look at the "lush field of life experience and limitless paths" photograph located on the previous page.

Close your eyes and envision yourself on the edge of this

lush field. This is a magical, mystical field. You feel the warmth of the rising sun, and you hear the wind dancing in the tall grass. In this field there are many paths and trails. There is only one path created especially for you, and it is unique to you. Now, enter the lush field and pause – you tune into your heart and allow your instinct to guide you directly to your own path.

You feel the gentle tickle of the tall grass brushing up against your thighs and occasionally you pause to turn yourself in a full circle to take in the abundant beauty that surrounds you in this environment. You can taste the sweetness in the air, the birds whisper their delight from the sky above you. The mountains beckon from behind the mist, as you peacefully plod along. You come upon a trail marker with your name written upon it. When you stand close to it, facing the sign, a path appears. Wow, you see and smell all your favourite trees, plants and flowers. Joyful, with a bounce in your step, you hop along the pathway, which opens up to an incredible clearing.

This is more than a clearing – it is in fact your very own personal nature sanctuary. A safe place that brings you great pleasure when you see it, and you feel calm when you hear the familiar sounds. Perhaps it is reminiscent of somewhere you loved to visit when you were a child, or a favourite travel destination. Right in the middle of your nature sanctuary is a dwelling. Excitedly, you approach the front entrance of the dwelling. You make your way to the door. There are special sensors on the door that are attuned to your essence and consequently the door opens automatically.

Inside the dwelling, there is a warm welcoming fire burning in the fireplace. You pause and appreciate all the comforts within this place and all there is for you to see, hear, and smell inside your dwelling, and you are so grateful. This is such a wonderful place. This is a special place that you can access at any time during the hike of life adventure. Meditation and your vivid imagination provide you with the ability to bend time and be in this place as often as you deem necessary. This is your sacred haven in the world.

I invite you to move over to the fireplace and stand with your back to the fire to warm yourself. Close your eyes and enjoy the physical sensations in your body in response to the warm, welcoming fire. Focus your attention on your heart-space and take a few deep, relaxing, cleansing breaths. You attune to the rhythm of your own heartbeat. You are so relaxed and comfortable in these peaceful surroundings. Your heart is miraculous indeed as it houses your eternal flame, your innate, divine inner light. You set your intention by saying silently to yourself, or out loud if it feels comfortable for you, "Way-shower, holy spirit, soul-self, inner light [or a different name that you consider suitable], go ahead of me and prepare the way for the hike of my life adventure."

As soon as the words have been expounded, you see a brilliant beam of light emanate from your heart-space across the floor, coming to rest in a stream of light upon a door. You walk within this beam of light to the door and with one hand you grasp the doorknob, while placing your other in the middle of the door. With the exact amount of pressure required, you turn the knob, push on the door, and it opens. Your inner light penetrates the shadow that was once behind the door and illuminates the space. When you remove your flat palm from the door a sign becomes visible upon the door: "The life experiences of _____," and your name is written there. This is your confirmation that this truly is your personal sacred sanctuary.

Pause now and be in this experience. There you are, standing with light streaming from your heart-centre and the door to your life experiences is open.

Check in with yourself and debrief the fact that the doorway is open to shine your innerlight upon your life experiences, which includes your secrets.

Do you feel any physical sensations in your body?
Is there any stirring of your emotions?
Is there anything visible to you within the stream of light?
What do you perceive?
Is there an aspect of your self there to greet you, from your childhood, adolescence, or adulthood?

Give yourself the gift of a few minutes to honor your individual process.

This door is always open now and the way is safe. On the hike of life adventure, you choose how you wish to beam your inner light. You choose the size of the light at any given moment, depending upon your willingness to see. You choose to bring that which is unconscious (in secret, in the dark shadow) into your conscious awareness (into the light beam). You can beam a pencil-thin flashlight beam, or a huge spotlight-sized beam. It is totally up to you how you light your way in a manner that is compatible and in a way of ease. You are comfortable, knowing that you manage the hike of life adventure process, the size and the intensity of your inner light, when you're ready to do so.

Make sure if there is an aspect of yourself whom you have acknowledged, that you assure them that you will be back again. You are not abandoning this aspect of self or saying goodbye – you are simply saying: "See you later". Affirm that you value their presence in your life and that you will be back often to this personal sanctuary, to listen and learn all that they have to share with you. When you feel complete, in the moment, you turn toward the fire and walk closer until you feel the warmth.

This is a very safe and magical fireplace. The fire is an eternal flame that is always lit, warm and welcoming for each visit to your own personal sacred sanctuary. You pause and enjoy the decor of your cherished mementos. You breathe in the beauty of this place, it will sustain you, with its unique sounds, sights, and smells. You take in a long slow inhalation and exhalation. What a glorious sanctuary. It's time now to leave this dwelling. As you approach the door it opens automatically and you exit. This truly is your very own personal sanctuary and you feel secure. Once outside, you marvel at the wonders contained within your nature sanctuary. You make your way to the wide familiar trail that brings you back to the lush field.

Debrief

Take time to answer these four questions before you continue.

What was the impact of this imagination exercise for you?

How did you feel when you took your flat hand off the door and saw the sign upon the interior door that read: "The life experiences of _____" with your name written on the door?

Did you experience any significant sensations in your physical body?

Did you sense or see anything in the stream of your inner light when brightness was cast into the dark shadow that was once behind the door?

Lush field of everyday life experience

Let me propose how this personal sanctuary may serve you in dealing effectively with real-life lessons in the lush field of everyday experience.

For instance, in your moving about in your daily interaction, a real-life event or circumstance pushes a button within you and you feel a reaction. In your silent observation of yourself you can say, "Isn't that interesting. I'm curious about this. I'd like to talk to myself about this point and see what this inner part of me wants to say."

This is a type of occasion when you can choose to imagine yourself within your personal sanctuary and talk with yourself: "Okay, I acknowledge this stimulation. I make time for you. I listen now for you. Tell me what it is you have to say." This is acknowledging rather than abandoning yourself, when your feeling nature has been stimulated. This is making a concerted, conscious effort to be available to yourself in new ways, rather than to betray the intuition of your feeling nature.

The reason for the stirring in a present day situation may be that there is some (past) hurt or (past) trauma that is coming up to be healed. It is as though the re-enactment in the present brings you to the edge and recalls a similar past event in order to free yourself from a limited way of perceiving, believing, thinking, or behaving.

Why? There may be unexpressed emotional energy attached to a past memory, which has been triggered by this current event. There is an aspect of yourself that needs to be seen, to be heard, to be acknowledged, and to be validated by you. Of course, you have the choice whether to feel, deal, and heal. It takes courage to move out of the comfort zone and habitual methods of using various distractions to resist the truth. There is a universal principle to consider when making your conscious choice to deal with any issue: "The lesson will be repeated until you learn the lesson." You either choose to feel, deal, and heal now or defer until later, knowing full well that it will come up again. Your question becomes: "Am I ready?" May I encourage you to say "Yes!"?

Here is an opportunity for you to invite this aspect of your self into your sanctuary in an imagination exercise. This is a method of using the gift of meditation to bend time to feel, deal, and heal a past experience. You have been triggered by an aspect of your self that is frozen in some past time-frame of experience and wants to reveal the truth to you now. This is what I mean by being available to yourself in new ways – giving yourself time and space to honor your feeling nature without betraying or abandoning yourself.

Making and keeping a brief daily appointment time with yourself, to meditate and visualize yourself in your personal sanctuary, may be the most precious gift you have ever given yourself. All it takes is practice. It doesn't matter how much time you give – yourself; it simply matters that there is some time for reflection and self-study – a process of making an investment in yourself, and there is no better investment.

If at any time you feel scared, take a good look at the letters in the word "scared." The same letters are used to create the word "sacred." Whenever you feel scared, you can honor the feeling and use the energy to transform it into a sacred inner connection, rather than reacting in fear and perpetuating your habit of creating an outer correction or distraction. Although this process may be new and seem strange, it is powerful for you as it enables you to take responsibility for your feeling nature in a constructive manner. You consciously honor your emotions, rather than being at their mercy when they are unconscious and wreak havoc in your life by destructively running the show.

When you make a sacred inner connection you may be dealing with the adult you were yesterday that was criticized at work, or the adolescent you were decades ago reliving an embarrassing moment, and/or even the child you once were that experienced some sort of trauma or abuse. During your inner connection time you bless yourself with increased self-understanding and enhanced self-awareness. Your experience will be unique to you.

Example – adult you were yesterday

Perhaps you completed a work project and anticipated some approval, recognition, or appreciation and you did not get it from external sources. You wanted acknowledgment and appreciation of your valuable contribution from those you work with, but there was none given. Perhaps you felt slighted, resentful, angry, and left work agitated. You kept yourself busy and distracted during the course of the evening and went to bed.

However, the next morning when it was time to get up and get ready to go to work, you did not feel motivated to do so. Your energy was very low. Your mind started rehearsing yesterday's events. Your anger, frustration, and feelings surfaced again. Now, your mind is off on a tangent and it pulls up a whole lot more from your past for you to nurse, curse, and rehearse. An entire string of tapes of similar experiences come out of storage from the backpack of burden, unhealed hurts that you've been denying and carrying.

So, now you can either continue this course of thought-action or you can stop and be available to yourself in new ways. You can say silently to yourself, or grab a journal and write in it, something like this: "Okay,_____ [put your name in the blank], what do you need? What do you want?" Now allow yourself time to respond. Sometimes non-dominant handwriting works well in this type of process.

To continue this example: "I need some recognition and appreciation of a job well done." Perhaps you silently say to the adult of yesterday, "Okay, I know you have learned in socializing and schooling that your work was graded and you were rewarded with marks and verbal praise for goals achieved and successful completions and a job well done. That served you then and quite obviously is not serving you now. Expecting acceptance, approval, appreciation, and recognition is normal. However, now you can be kind to yourself by giving it to yourself, rather than waiting for it to come from others external to yourself. This is now an inside job and it is for you to honor your intrinsic value. The bonus of learning to honor and value yourself is that it will become natural to honor and value others, and this will be returned to you through limitless and unexpected relationship sources."

This may resolve and provide opportunity for you to be seen, heard, acknowledged, and validated with regard to yesterday's events. However, it may take a few days, weeks, months, even years, to proceed through the entire string of events that were triggered and recalled as a consequence of yesterday's events. The past events were recalled because it is likely that there is an energetic charge of unexpressed emotion attached to each event that needs to be honored by you and allowed to run its course. This is an opportunity for you to daily stop by your personal sanctuary, have a date with yourself, and allow your process to evolve.

All that is required of you is to make time and create an opportunity to feel the suppressed emotions and allow them to run their course by expressing them in the most compatible way possible. Write in a journal, squeeze sponge-rubber stress balls, jump on a rebounder (mini-trampoline), go for a jog, do some sketching, write a poem or a song, hum or chant... Consciously deal with the issue by acknowledging its existence and endeavoring to determine the limiting root core belief that no longer serves you. Heal the past wound or burden by being available to yourself, and stop abandoning yourself by denying your needs and wants. Reveal to yourself the truth of the actual events. A wonder-filled process of being "response-able" for your thoughts, feelings, actions, results, attitudes, behaviors, and beliefs. A systematic process of taking responsibility for the consequences of all of the aforementioned. You may also decide to choose an appropriate counselor so you are not alone in your process and you can receive some expert guidance, encouragement, and support.

Example – adolescent you were years ago

Perhaps, in your adolescent years, you became progressively self-conscious of your body due to shaming comparisons and remarks made by media, peers, parents, siblings, relatives, or passers-by. Each time it happened you laughed along with the group with those about you, while inside you were crying. The comparisons eroded your self-esteem. You took these messages to heart as truth, and began to believe they were true. Not only did you believe them to be true, you internally berated yourself and reminded yourself. Then, one day, someone makes a comment and you overreact. Their comment was the last straw. The overreaction is a result of the accumulation of years of limiting beliefs about self that are not even yours, but beliefs that you adopted from others. The gift of the stimulation is to discern the truth for yourself and free yourself from the past limiting beliefs and comments of others that very obviously are not life-giving and supportive to you in the present.

When the adolescent you comes forward, it's important to acknowledge that this may not entail a simple dialogue. This may be the beginning of a process that will evolve from your willingness to be available to your adolescent self. Invest time in yourself and invite the adolescent you to your sanctuary, and allow it to be seen, heard, acknowledged, and validated by you. Allow the adolescent to tell you the true story of the life they lived to an open receptive audience – you the adult. If you decide that it would be beneficial to also have some professional assistance, then seek it. It is not a sign of weakness to ask for help. We inhabit a planet with over six billion people. We are here to help each other, to learn, to grow, to assist and support one another.

Example – the child you once were

Let's assume that on a visit to your sanctuary, you see the child you once were huddled behind the door of your life experience. Your child is afraid of the bright light that has consumed their hiding place, and afraid of this sudden interest from you, the adult of the present. You may wish to begin your acquaintance with your child-self with a dialogue with the child that goes something like this.

"Hello, dear one. I'm here to give you permission to express whatever it is you wish to express. It's okay to be emotional, here, now, with me. I understand that in the past permission was not granted by those about you for you to express your emotionality, your opinions, and your stories. Adults in your life were overburdened with too many responsibilities to be able to administer love and compassion. Also, it is possible that the adults in your life back then had never had it modeled to them and therefore they did not even know how to care for their own emotional and psychological needs. Maybe you were scolded at times and grew up believing that 'children are to be seen and not heard,' and I understand if you're hesitant to speak with me now. Big people did not have time for little people in the past. Although I am a big person, I have the time and I have the knowledge that I wish to put into practice. I'm here to help you. I honor the essence of child that you are and I desire to develop a rapport with you now."

The child may not trust you, as this process is new and different and strange. The child may not trust this sudden change. You see, children are spontaneous, not controllers and planners like adults. You may need to apologize to your child aspect of self and say that you're sorry: "I'm so sorry that adults did not give you the time or attention that you needed in your very young years. I'm sorry you felt as though you were in the way, a burden, or a nuisance. I'm so sorry you felt abandoned and ignored and adopted the limiting belief that you were unworthy of love and support, and that you had to cope with things on your own in isolation that were overwhelming and confusing for a child."

The child may say, " Why this sudden interest now?"

Then you, the adult, could respond with something like this: "I wish to acknowledge that all of my life experience is of value; you are of value. I promise you that I will never punish you or abandon you again. I'll believe you, whatever it is you have to tell me. Your secrets are safe with me. I love all aspects of you. You are a precious child of God, innocent, radiantly beautiful, and I love you totally and completely. Whatever you need to assist you with your healing, I'll make arrangements for you or provide it for you myself. Whenever we make appointments for professional help or support, I will explain the process to you. I'll tell you where we are going and approximately how long we will be there, so that you will not be afraid of these new big people. This is a process, and there is no rush. I know it may take a considerable time for you to tell me the true story of the life you lived. I am here for you and I am committed to healing the trauma you have experienced. I know you have carried a burden for a very long time. You are no longer alone in coping with it. I am here and willing to listen, so you can express your repressed, suppressed, and stored emotional energy. The reason I know this is because if there were no emotional charge attached to these memories, I would not have reacted and been stimulated in the way I have been today. I ask and invite you to tell me what it is you have to say."

How the child aspect of self will express itself will be unique. This is a process of being kind to self and trusting the impulses within you to do particular things, watch certain movies, buy crayons and draw, make spontaneous sounds, music and movements, or simply be and allow the cleansing, healing tears to flow. It is a commitment you make to take your own hand outstretched from within your own heart and say, "I'm here for you, no matter what!" A commitment to stop by your personal sanctuary daily to dialogue with yourself about issues as they come forward to you.

Perhaps dialogue with yourself is not the most compatible form of expression for you. The child aspect of your self may instead choose to reveal the truth of their experience to you by printing in a journal, speaking with a noble friend, going to your spiritual advisor, a personal coach, a counselor, or a psychologist. It's wonderful to give yourself the gift of support. There is great reward in having a witness during your intensely personal sacred healing journey. A witness is someone who agrees to support you by being an open-hearted listener. They are a non-judgmental audience who will listen when you need to be seen, heard, acknowledged, and validated. They do not take on the problem, nor do they try to change you or fix the issue. Their job is to listen and to be a sounding-board, to allow you to talk it all out until you come to the logical next step or simply the place of peace and resolution with the matter at hand.

The most compatible form of expression is for you to decide. It may not be the same each time you connect with your child in your sanctuary. It matters not how, it matters only that you tell yourself the truth and honor and respect yourself. This is the process where your knowledge becomes understanding, wisdom, and compassion through experience of all aspects of self.

Example – Strategy for an inopportune time to be completely available to self

It's important to note that, in your interaction and moving about in your daily life, you may receive stimulation that triggers a past event at an inopportune time. Please do not compound the destructive habit of resistance or denial of your feeling nature. Consciously acknowledge the stimulation in silence by saying to yourself, "I acknowledge there is a message, for I have received and I accept this prompting from within me as a result of my interaction with this person, place, or thing. I acknowledge this stimulation and my reaction. I must postpone this slightly, for I am not in a position to take or make time to be available to myself at present. I am currently at work, or driving, in a meeting, engaged in a sporting activity, or shopping. However, I will be home at _____ [time] and I will make myself available then."

This is putting in place a system of support to give yourself. This is building a rapport with yourself that honors and respects your commitment to feel, deal, heal, and reveal your personal past. This is providing an opportunity to free yourself from being a prisoner of your past pain. An agreement you make with yourself that is life-giving and loving.

Personal story

When my child aspect came forward to me within my sanctuary, it was a process that spanned a number of months. Obviously, this aspect of my child had plenty to tell me. I wish to point out here, though, that it took weeks before my child would speak. At first, it would just come to the sanctuary and watch and study me. It did not trust me. When there was a level of comfort for the child, the child came close to me and would test me, to see if I would react and scold or raise a hand to harm the child. Slowly the child ventured nearer and one day it came to sit next to me in the sanctuary and the story began to unfold and the healing process evolved. By the way, so did the furnishings in the sanctuary. My child wanted a rocking chair, and a thick sheepskin rug to snuggle in by the fireplace. So these things were added during the imagination exercise.

In my case there was the verbal storytelling, there was emotional release, there was physical movement, and there was drawing. I experienced flashbacks of past events with incredible detail and specificity. Everything came forward to me in a gentle, compatible manner and I was never given more in one session than I could deal with. I was guided to particular individuals who assisted me by sharing their respective gifts and talents with regards to holistic healing therapies, books, audio cassettes, videos, live lectures, courses, support groups, spiritual retreats, counselors, and medical professionals. Also, the child would at times ask for things to assist with the healing journey. I was prompted to purchase particular music and children's movies that would assist me to get in touch with my feeling nature, and a plastic baseball bat and a rebounder so the child could safely express physical energy. When expressing anger energy, the plastic baseball bat was used to hit and strike objects so the energy could move down my arms. Then when the energy wanted to express itself through my legs, I was guided to lean my rebounder up against a sofa in a vertical position so I could kick it. Other times, I would be out walking and be prompted to kick a chain-link fence. This was in addition to the punching of pillows and punch-bags. I experienced physical, emotional, vocal, and creative energy expressions.

The process is miraculous indeed, and you will experience your own intensely personal sacred healing journey through the hike of life adventure.

When your child aspect of self is complete in the story-telling

Next is an imagination/meditation exercise to bring into the present the essence of the child aspect of your self that was frozen in some past time-frame of experience. Once the child aspect of yourself is complete in the storytelling phase of the process, this exercise will bring the energy of the child that was frozen in a past time-frame of experience into present-day time with you today.

Envision behind your closed eyes the image you as the child storyteller, standing a few feet away from you the adult and facing you. Focus on the heart-space of this child image of you. See a brilliant light radiating from the heart of the child, which then becomes a luminescent liquid flowing in a stream from the heart-space of this child, into the heart-space of you the adult. As the energy flows out of the child aspect of self that was frozen in the past time-frame of experience, and into the adult aspect of self in the present time, the image of the child falls away like a ragdoll. Once you are complete in the reception of this energy you may feel differently in your body. It may feel as though the energy actually clicks into place and then expands throughout your body.

Once you have dissolved the separation between the adult you and the child you, the integration may surprise and bless you. You may remember and be inclined to have play-days more often. You may do things more spontaneously. You may be prompted to buy things purely for comfort and delight, such as things that sparkle, fleece clothing, new socks, sneakers, caps, new quilt, more pillows, candles, new music, new lighting fixtures, or new home furnishings. You may rekindle your interest in certain activities and visit a sporting goods store to purchase gear so you can go out and do things you haven't done for a long time, or sign up for ski, swim, archery, golf, bowling, horseriding, guitar, or piano. You may not be such a fanatic about keeping the house or your vehicle so clean. You may find a huge shift in your priorities. You may simplify your life. You may take long bubble baths rather than quick showers. You may purchase stuffed animals or rubber ducks. You may throw away the hectic schedule. You may go barefoot or walk in the rain purely for the pleasure of the tactile stimulation. You may take naps or go golfing more often. You may take more frequent mini-vacations. Who knows, until you've invested the time in yourself and given yourself the gift of awareness and self-study development.

You may gain conscious access to other child aspects of self that have not expressed themselves very much in your adult life. Although the wounded aspect of self may have been running the show, you may experience appearances of the playful, the spontaneous, the vulnerable, the magical, the wonder, the intuitive, the creative, or the wise owl, to name a few. Drs. Hal and Sidra Stone in their psychology book *Embracing Our Selves* describe what they see is a psychology of selves within each of us. There are many aspects of self that compose our personality, each with a distinctive energetic expression. Their leading-edge work explains "voice dialogue," a technique that helps to increase our awareness and understanding of the various aspects of self as we gain conscious access through experience.

When you literally lighten your load of past excess baggage, you open the way, you open the door and receive the surprise of that which comes into the light. Using our imagination in a meditative process truly is a gift, as it provides us with the ability to bend time in order to feel, deal, heal, and reveal our personal past. We free ourselves from being the prisoners of the pain of our past. We can create and thrive in the now, rather than merely coping, carrying the burden of our personal past as excess emotional baggage, and just surviving.

I encourage you to be kind to yourself by making and keeping a daily appointment to meet with yourself to develop a rapport relationship. Be gentle with yourself. Be patient with this whole new way of relating to, and being available to, yourself. Here's an example of a possible commitment intention to make with yourself.

> "I hereby commit to set aside time each day before my sleep time to give myself and to be available to myself in new ways. I intend to keep this agreement with myself."

What about when something comes up that you thought you'd already dealt with?

When you have something come up that you thought you'd already dealt with, it is simply that a deeper clearing is perhaps required. Rather than being frustrated or angry, support yourself by asking the following questions.

> "What is this about?"
> "How far through the levels have I moved?"
> "Have I gotten to the depth of it?"
> "Is this residue of a physical, intellectual, emotional, energetic, spiritual, psychological, or physiological nature?
> "What is it that is wanting conscious acknowledgment and expression in my hike of my life adventure?"
> "What do I need to surrender – a limiting thought, an attitude, a behavior, or a limiting root core belief?"

By the way, surrender is not a passive giving up. Surrender, as described by Janet Quinn in an article and shared by

Larry Dossey in his book *Healing Words*, "is being extraordinarily involved in one's process. It doesn't mean once and for all. It means time and time again. Over and over until one experiences freedom from the limitation being surrendered."

Pause for a moment and honor the child within by reading the following poem.

What child is this within me?

What child is this within me,
That clearly calls for spontaneity?
What child is this within me,
That expresses such vulnerability?
What child is this within me,
That desires bonding and into me see?
What child is this within me,
That forgives and accepts unconditionally?
What child is this within me,
That co-creates for eternity?
How, how do I allow
This delicate essence to guide me?
Now, now I choose to surrender,
And trust this child, "I am."
And trust this child, this essence,
"I am."

Breakaway Experiences

Imagination exercise

I invite you to imagine yourself on the opposite side of the lush field, far from the pink blossoming flower. You are just under the damp mist that clings to the slope of the mountain range. From your position you hear the distinctive, yet distant, sound of the ocean. You must follow the outer perimeter of the lush field to pick up a trail that hugs the baseline of the mountain. The landscape changes dramatically and you enter a totally different ecosystem. Your heartbeat quickens and your step lightens in the anticipation and excitement of seeing new sights as your adventure continues. You smell the sea and even taste the sea salt on your lips. When you round the next corner you come out of the trees to an expanse of beach below you. From this vantage point your eyes focus upon a large sandstone monolith that is being lapped from all sides by the surging waves of the mighty ocean. The waves demand your full attention and turbulently swirl inside and fill the tunnel they have carved within the monolith. You are captivated by this piece of the earth that has broken away. Your intuition guides each step you take in the direction of this breakaway section of sandstone. You quickly surmise that it will be possible for you to safely make your way down to a protected cove in close proximity to the breakaway. As you near the spot you have selected to make your safe descent, you discover some primitive steps and natural rock stairs. As you descend, you pause frequently for rest and relaxation in this new environment.

Eventually you find yourself standing on the shore, and you're in awe of the huge sandstone structure that has broken off from the mainland. You ponder for a moment, asking yourself the following questions.

"What is the symbolism of this breakaway to me?"

"Could it be an invitation to consider that, as I venture through life, it is necessary to break away from particular people, places, possessions, or positions?"

"Is nature giving me a nudge to release and free myself from an identity that no longer serves me?"

"Am I being called to pay attention to my habitual ways of thinking, acting, behaving, and believing and to break away from that which I determine is no longer life-giving?"

Pause, and take a few deep breaths before you continue reading. To clear your mind and honor what may have been stimulated within, take time for inner connection and jot down some of your initial impulses, thoughts, or perceptions.

Breakaway in a change of people, places, possessions, or positions – a relocation analogy

Creating a support system requires an enormous investment of time and patience. A move of house can shake you up and out of your comfort zones, and into an identity crisis. Where you formerly had an established career, a regular routine, local hang-outs, and a weekly schedule, it is a shock to your system to have absolutely everything changed. I have befriended many individuals in their grief over the loss, due to distance, of all that was familiar. It is important for those of us who are the locals to open and welcome the new arrivals, knowing that we and they can learn so much from each other. Just think of all the new cultures to explore, new foods to sample, new games to play, new prayers to pray, and new friendships to cultivate and nurture.

Brave, bold woman story

I have had the privilege to meet many new Canadians. I'd like to share one story. This woman initially began corresponding through letter-writing to a male friend of a co-worker of her aunt. A relationship blossomed and after two years her Canadian correspondent visited the Philippines, where she lived. Within a short time they were married and a year later she emigrated to Canada. In her native country she was a respected teacher with a remarkable track record. She was an internationally trained professional and her teaching degree was not initially honored in Canada. She applied herself and took university courses to prove her value and upgrade her qualifications in the hope of resuming her teaching career in Canada. Although she passed all the classes with flying colors, she was faced with the bitter reality of racial prejudice.

An important point to make here is that, just because an individual has a unique way of speaking, which our ears are not attuned to, it does not mean they are not fluent in the English language. This woman had taught all her classes in English even though the school was in the Philippines. In order to earn a living as a new Canadian she took nanny jobs and babysitting jobs to make an income, and pressed on with hope in her heart of one day being a teacher in Canada.

Through a series of circumstances, she was offered a job providing customer service in a restaurant. This certainly was not her ambition in life. Sometimes we must work to meet our basic needs while taking actionable steps in the direction of our dreams. This job also assisted her in building her self-confidence in her new country and learning more about the culture. Can you imagine a demure, polite Filipino woman learning the social nuances of workmen and professionals in a semi-rural farming community? What an opportunity to learn about the idiosyncrasies of Canadian culture and language first-hand.

The business was sold in less than a year and luckily she had some great encouragement. The idea was given to her to do some voluntary work in the local schools close to her home, seeing that she did not drive. She did hundreds of hours of voluntary work and was even given an opportunity to write and present some lesson plans to the students. She requested reference letters from the principals and the classroom teachers. She invited the powers-that-be to come and observe her in the classroom environment, and successfully presented lessons to the class. Finally, she was granted the privilege to teach in Canada and has been active in her chosen profession for almost a decade. She has blossomed and grown in her new environment; she learned to drive and has purchased a car and a home.

There are many stories about real people in their trials, tribulations, and challenges when it comes to breaking away from their birthplace to emigrate to a new land. Immigrants are remarkable individuals with incredible stories to tell us, if we choose to break away from our limited preconceived ideas, our racial prejudices, and our ethnical misconceptions. People in our global family have been displaced due to the ravages of war and a wide variety of other reasons. Some choose a new country, while others are refugees. I encourage you to risk introducing yourself to any new member of our global family that has relocated to your community – and treasure the experience. It will surely bless you with the opportunity to realize how much you take for granted if you have always lived in the same country or community. You never know who will inspire you to follow your heart and create your dream!

New perception

What about using the above example as a springboard to making desired changes in your life without changing everything? That would be much easier to cope with, wouldn't it? I encourage you to take some time to scan your current lifestyle, the people, places, possessions, positions, identities you assume. Are they life-giving? Do they feed you, inspire you, and enrich you? Are you coping (just surviving) or creating and thriving?

These are profound questions to ponder, which will surely bless you with abundant opportunities to create what you say is most important to you. For simplicity, let's say a wholesome, balanced lifestyle is composed of basically four quadrants: health, wealth, career, and relationships. If you desire to make a personal positive change in one of these four quadrants, which would be your number-one priority at this time? Is it your health, which includes physical, emotional, spiritual, and psychological wellness? Is it your wealth, your career, or your relationships?

I was asked this question during an introductory session of a course I was considering. I invite you to ask yourself this question and fill in the blank with the area you have selected as your priority: "Based on results, in this area of my life, _____ [fill in the blank with the area you wish to experience different results be it health, wealth, career, or relationships]. How can I continue to have the same thoughts, attitudes, behaviors, or beliefs about _____ and expect a different result?" This is a way of saying: "If there is no change, there is no change." This is opening to the notion that all thoughts are energy, and thoughts as energy directly affect experiences of life.

Example – personal health

To demonstrate the aforementioned point I say to myself: "Based on the results that I am currently experiencing in my health, how can I continue negative self-talk and over-eating and expect a different result?" When I tell myself the truth I identify my limitation. Then I am free to create new thoughts that are accepting, and research how to create a balanced, wholesome, healthy action plan. Also, I can learn how to honor my feelings and emotions by feeling them rather than feeding them. I can seek outside assistance and support to create my desired changes. I can pay close attention to my thoughts and feelings about myself. I can determine when I reach for food: "Am I eating to satisfy true hunger or am I eating as a temporary distraction from honoring my emotions?" I can observe my thoughts, attitudes, behaviors, and beliefs that inhibit the manifestation of radiant vital health. I can create a new program of life-giving self-talk, emotional expression, and self-managment.

This is a self-observation tool (the question), that can be used to enhance self-understanding and increase self-awareness, when you identify for yourself that you're stuck. How do you know when you're stuck? When you're impatient, frustrated, depressed, living on automatic pilot, when you can say to yourself: "I've been in this place before and I don't like the discontent"? It is at times like this that you empower yourself and ask the question. It provides space to stop and discern what it is that no longer serves. Is it my thoughts, attitudes, behaviors, or beliefs I need to break-away from in order to create the desired changes and work toward a new and different result?

Has your heart been giving you little hints to break away from a grueling routine that you really do not enjoy any more? Is there a call from within you that desires more mini-timeouts? Do you desire to break away from habitual ways of "doing" life, to create a more fulfilling, simpler lifestyle? When was the last time you actually did what you love to do? Do you even know what that is?

Exercise

Take a fresh sheet of paper and draw a line vertically down the centre. On one side of the paper create a list of all the activities that you have ever said that you enjoy doing or experiencing. Opposite each entry on the other side of the paper, note the last time that you actually did that which you claim to like to do or experience. Below is an example.

Dancing	1 year ago
Downhill skiing	4 years ago
Golfing	10 years ago
Artistic painting	3 years ago
Volleyball	5 years ago
Camping	4 years ago
Picnic in the park with the kids	4 years ago
Ice-skating	15 years ago
Reading a book for entertainment	10 years ago
Basketball	20 years ago
Bicycle-riding	7 years ago
Hosting a dinner party	3 years ago
Going out on a date	9 years ago
Attending a live musical production/ play	2 years ago

This type of self-questioning is a wake-up call to realize the last time that you actually did what you like. Recreation time simply for the pure joy of it. Are you so focused on achieving results that you have forgotten that your life is to be lived and enjoyed? When was it that you lost touch with yourself? When was it that you lost yourself in your work or family? When was it you began to exist on automatic pilot to pay the bills without leaving time and space for balance and fun in your life? Is there a better time than the present to be reacquainted with, or to get to know, yourself, perhaps for the first time in your life? One pretty reliable meter that indicates when you're doing something you truly love to do is that you lose all track of time.

This is a simple method of learning to attune to, and develop trust in, your own heart as it speaks to you. Your heart is your divine connection to Spirit. Your heart knows your truth far more than you give yourself credit for. Far, far more. When you reconnect with what you love to do and begin to do it, you feel alive and passionate about life. When you live passionately your energy level surges upward from the aliveness of your soul. Who knows, you may decide that living your passions is so rewarding and satisfying that they become your next career.

Exercise

I invite you to scan your life and recall times when you made decisions that were out of alignment with your heart. Did you come to know stress, strain, and struggle as a consequence of making a decision contrary to the wisdom and prompting of your heart?

Now scan your life and recall times when you made decisions that were in alignment with your heart. Did you feel as though you were in flow and that it was the way of ease?

Allow me to clarify that the way of ease does not mean the way of no work. The way of ease means that you have your heart to guide you, working together with your mind in order to advance each other, rather than your heart and your mind working to the exclusion of each other.

The lesson to glean from this scanning of your life is certainly not to be an exercise where you beat yourself up. It is simply to clarify and demonstrate to yourself that you have choice, and that you are very wise. You clearly know the difference between the way of stress, strain, and struggle and the way of ease which is in flow, in alignment with, the heart of truth within you, as it guides you. With your increased self-understanding and awareness, I bet that you effect some life-giving changes in your life.

Breakaway analogy in a health-related example

Using the breakaway analogy, let's relate it to a health crisis or medical challenge. It is important to listen to the diagnosis given to you by your team of healthcare professionals. It is equally important to combine the professional diagnosis with your own research and exploration. Your wise guidance knows what resonates true for you. Who knows your body better than you do? After all, you have inhabited it, you think the thoughts within it, you know your emotional state, you know your personal history, you know your spiritual beliefs, and you know your likes and dislikes.

I encourage you to be a co-participant in your health challenge or crisis, fully to whatever degree that you can. Be eclectic, draw and learn from multiple sources that resonate with you. Be a co-creator during your healing path or medical challenge/crisis. There are beneficial attributes to traditional medicine practices and holistic healthcare practices. The wholeness of self includes health of the physical, intellectual, emotional, energetic, physiological, psychological, and spiritual aspects of the personage.

Personal example

I experienced the healing path of remedial surgery. I asked my surgeon to partner with me in utilizing an idea that Dr. C. Northrop shared in her book Women's Bodies Women's Wisdom. (There are beneficial ideas in her book that men and women can use when preparing for surgery, recovering from it, and as part of your ongoing healing journey.) I requested that my surgeon read a page of affirmative statements I'd prepared before she conduct the surgical procedure. I requested that she partner with me in consciousness, meaning that she was willing to share and support my intentions while performing the surgery. I also requested the document be read to me while going under anesthesia, during the procedure, and upon conclusion of the process. To create as comforting an environment as possible, considering the invasive surgery procedure, I asked the medical team to play in the operating room a CD I'd brought from home.

   This was certainly a breakaway from past surgery experiences. Emergency surgery, of course, does not allow you to plan like this. However, you may find other beneficial ideas in Dr. Northrop's book to assist and support yourself through the recovery and rehabilitation phase.

Boosting the immune system

Regarding my health, I prepared myself for eight months prior to my two-year journey around the world. I was referred to a bio-kineseologist, a herbalist, an iridologist, and a homeopath. The bio-kineseologist introduced me to vibrational healing techniques, which provided me with knowledge that became understanding through experience of myself as an intricate system of energy. She also showed me how to use a pendulum. Using the pendulum, or dowsing, is also called divining. The most proficient dowsers have a very clear understanding that the connection to the infinite field of all possibilities is not separate from us. The magnetic forcefield is the carrier of vital forces that are always flowing through us. In dowsing we are directing energy with the power of thought and flipping a mental switch to "turn on" and open up our access to our higher-self for direction. The pendulum is a crutch that you can use until you develop more attunement with your physical body and more clarity in the energetic dynamic of your being.

Personal example

I purchased a metal pendulum suspended on a short chain approximately two to three inches long. Holding the chain between my thumb and middle finger so the pendulum dangled, I asked, "Please show me a 'yes' response" and I waited for the pendulum to react and respond. The next step was to ask for a "no" response. I was advised that this is a simple yet effective tool that will provide me with clarity. It is not a tool to use as a fortune-telling device. It is a crutch to use until you develop your attunement with your innate capability to allow your physical self to assist in providing you with more clarity, after which point you will no longer need a pendulum. Once you remember and develop your innate sensitivity to subtle energy, you can receive your answers intuitively.

Before you dowse at any time, it is important to ask your higher-self for permission. "Can I, may I, should I dowse at this time?" I used the pendulum to dowse a long list of foods to create a life-giving nutrition plan for myself. This was certainly a breakaway from the traditional food and nutrition guide I was introduced to in my youth. I no longer focused on simply a protein, dairy, starch, fruits and vegetable model. I had been on every commercial diet on the market with the intent of losing weight in an attempt to buy my self-worth because it was attached to my body image. I had never before considered eating for energetic vitality with the intent of boosting and building my immune system. A couple of great resources are a book by Paul Pitchford entitled *Healing with Whole Foods – Oriental Traditions and Modern Nutrition,* and another by Drs. Phyllis and James Balch entitled *Prescription for Dietary Wellness – Using Foods to Heal.*

Another aspect of breakaway with regard to creating a customized nutrition action plan for yourself is to consider the color of the foods, herbs, and spices you utilize. I have found for myself that when I eat particular foods my body has very specific reactions to certain food sources. I found that I can eat red, yellow, and orange peppers and feel great, but when I eat green peppers I have a different, less pleasant, experience. I find that when I eat apples with red skin my body reacts differently than when I eat apples with green skin. My body seems to prefer aduki or anasazi beans to other varieties. I use red, orange, or white lentils more readily than green, yellow, or brown. I have more energy when I eat quinoa, brown basmati rice, and bread or pasta made from kamut or spelt flours, as opposed to other grains and wheat products.

There are so many things I have learned from paying attention to how I feel after eating, which have contributed to making different choices for myself with respect to my personal nutrition action plan. I must admit, though, that I progressed very well for a couple years and then fell back into the old familiar ways of eating. When I paid attention to eating for energy, my physical self was more radiant, slim, trim, and vibrant. I had more energy to work a healthy action plan (exercise) and my body loved it. I have experienced both ends of the spectrum – being very fit and being very overweight. For me it seemed that I needed to experience both ends of the spectrum and make new and different choices as I endeavor to create a balanced nutrition action plan and an effective healthy action plan. I cultivated new life-giving habits for a time and then, after a couple years, digressed into old familiar patterns.

I learned that I could radically improve my overall health with a parasite cleanse and an appropriate nutrition action plan, while simultaneously working on my spiritual, energetic, psychological, and emotional wellness. My body responded rapidly to this new approach to health. In my research and self-study I learned that I could choose whether to take the long list of immunizations recommended for travelers going to the particular regions on the earth that I would visit. I had been told all my life that I was sensitive. This is very true. On an energetic level, I am ultrasensitive and was so totally paranoid for two weeks, after having just two inoculations in the doctor's office, I chose not to have any more. I am not recommending that you do not take immunizations when traveling about the globe. I made a choice for myself based upon my unique healthy action and nutrition plan. I was under strict constitutional homeopathic care to the degree that I believed I had strengthened my immune system to optimum vitality. Immunization is a choice you are free to make after careful consideration, consultation with your healthcare team, and time invested in adequately boosting up your immune system.

More than basic anatomy

I cannot believe how ignorant I was with regards to how my own body works. I had never invested time or energy to learn about the role of each organ and the various systems that are contained within my internal environment, which obviously contribute to my overall health and wellbeing. When various holistic healthcare practitioners made reference to things like the adrenals, endocrine system, lymph nodes, sympathetic and autonomic nervous systems, thyroid gland, pineal, pituitary, etc., it was foreign to me. I had no idea what they were talking about, let alone that I had them inside my body. This is more than the basic anatomy I learned in school. Through research and questioning holistic healthcare practitioners and healthcare professionals, I am still learning about the foods and herbs that support optimum health, and how my body actually functions.

Is it important to you to understand what nutrients your body requires? What nutrients the body produces itself? Of the nutrients that the body requires, what are those it requires from food intake? Which of those from food intake come from animal substances and plant substances and supplementation?

Personal example

From two different holistic healthcare practitioners, I learned that my lymphatic system was severely congested. I had no idea that the lymph system is actually larger than the blood vessel system. To learn more I consulted *Anatomy Coloring Workbook* by I. Edward Alcamo, Ph.D. In this book it states: "The lymphatic system is a series of vessels, structures, organs that collect fluid throughout the body and return it to the main circulation for redistribution. The system also contains cells known as lymphocytes, which function in the immune process." I was amazed to learn that there are sixteen different types of lymph nodes involved in the drainage of the head alone, not to mention the rest of the system. I learned that lymphatic congestion is closely related to emotional congestion.

Are you willing to entertain the notion that a common cold could be part of a lymphatic cleanse or emotional clearing process? I encourage you to explore and research if you feel inspired to do so; you will learn volumes and this will indeed empower you to create a healthy action and nutrition plan. In the past I depended solely upon my family doctor with regard to healthcare. What about you? Are you willing to take a more response-able approach to your optimum health and overall wellbeing? Are you willing to create a healthy action and nutrition plan for yourself?

Body as a system of energy

What about breaking away from the idea that the body is a vehicle, to considering it to be an intricate system of energy? I learned and practiced some basic t'ai chi (a gift to the world from China). I learned and practiced reiki (a gift to the world from Japan). I learned and practiced hatha yoga and pranayama (gifts to the world from India). I learned edgu (therapeutic and evolutionary spinal maintenance). I learned through experience about acupuncture, a new method of chiropractic care, reflexology, homeopathy, breathwork or vivation, cranial sacral, muscle testing, watsu water therapy, various types of massage, color therapy, and aromatherapy. I will not give you a description of all of these things, but if you're attracted to any of them, then it is for you to do your own quality control test and discover through experience what resonates with you and is beneficial to you.

Personal experience

I would like to share with you how doing my personal investigation through experience changed my perception of yoga. My initial reaction to yoga was: "Who wants to sit on the ground and imitate being a pretzel cooked in the

squat?" While living at an ashram in India it was compulsory
to do two one-hour classes of hatha yoga each day. I learned
that "ha" means sun and "tha" means moon. I really enjoyed
dynamic hatha yoga called "surya namaskara," which is a
series of twenty-four movements. I also learned that a stiff
body physically represents stiff thinking. I could certainly
relate to the word "stiff." I was invited by the instructor to
imagine my body to be a sponge. The postures are a way of
twisting and squeezing the sponge. By holding a posture
one brings conscious awareness to the body, so we can
isolate and tune into our current limitation. Yoga for me
became a process of asking my body, "Why am I unable to
complete or hold this posture? How do I feel in this
posture? What is the source of my limitation? What is my
limiting thought or belief?" Through this process I
addressed many limiting beliefs and realized how much I
have abused my own body.

For years I have struggled and strained to achieve
results. In the past I had played competitive softball and the
number of times I threw myself on the ground to slide into
a base or homeplate are too numerous to mention. Why? To
achieve a result, to score a run, to win a game, without conscious consideration of the long-term consequences of bat-
tering my body. In hindsight, what I once called sport and
considered exercise and fun is ludicrous to me now.

During one yoga class I was particularly frustrated and at
the end of the class the instructor had us all roll over on the
floor, lay flat on our backs on our yoga mats, and close our
eyes. He was pretty intuitive and during this relaxation meditation he said, "When one wishes someone, somewhere, or
something to be other than it is, one is unhappy." My chest
began to heave as I succumbed to my emotion. As I cried,

my tears streamed from my eyes right into my ears. I had been so frustrated and so unhappy with my body, because I had been comparing myself to others in the class who had slim bodies and were so much more flexible than I. I realized how my own comparison thoughts created my frustration and further eroded my self-esteem. I had long practiced this habit of comparison and had finally, silently admitted to myself that I had unrealistic expectations of myself. I really hated that I wasn't slim, trim, fit, firm, and flexible, and I hated my body. It was this attitude toward myself that was causing my frustration. I vowed to myself, "No more struggling and straining to achieve results!" I even saw a road sign to affirm my new resolve: "Be gentle, no my curves." I did have two good chuckles, one for the sign spelled incorrectly and one for the message I perceived, as if my body was talking to me "be gentle, know my curves."

I realized that I had lived the first two decades of my life totally invested in the physical and intellectual aspects of the personage, without giving too much conscious consideration to the emotional, energetic, physiological, psychological, or spiritual aspects. It was certainly a breakaway experience when I began to consider that there is more to life, and to me, than the intellectual and the physical. The quest to know and understand all aspects of myself has been such a rewarding evolution. I encourage you to dedicate yourself to lifelong learning and imagine that the best is yet to come. There is so much to explore and experience to create a wholesome, balanced, harmonious, life-giving lifestyle.

Breakaway analogy in a wealth example

I started working so I could buy things. I enhanced my career by taking night courses, putting in the long hours, setting goals, being proactive, a "human doing", achieving to create a comfortable lifestyle. Many years were invested in order to possess a home, a car, and furnishings, and to achieve success by outer material appearances. Yes, I was externally successful, yet internally empty. My breakaway experience came via a sporting accident that definitely changed my lifestyle.

I had been living in the fast lane, working downtown, working hard, and using drugs and alcohol to numb and/or relax. The injury I sustained was a wake-up call – my spiritual nature wanting conscious acknowledgment. I had six months to contemplate life during my recovery process. Talk about forced soul-searching. Now I view the injury as my lifesaver, a divine redirection of my life. I changed careers, met new friends, and began to invest time in my journey of faith. My life of self-destructive behavior was brought to an abrupt halt, and I entered into the process of learning to follow my heart and take steps to create what it is I now say is rewarding and satisfying. I'm not suggesting that you need a crisis to make changes. Part of the hike of my life adventure was to know the extremes in order to effect a balance somewhere in between.

Is there a longing within you for "something more"? Have you exhausted yourself trying to satisfy this longing through external corrections? Did it ever occur to you that your spiritual aspect of self wants bonding and intimacy with you through innerconnection.

Breakaway analogy in a career-related example

Using breakaway analogy, let's relate it to a career crisis. When corporate restructuring necessitates a lay-off and you find yourself without a job, there may be shock, grief, anger, and/or relief, depending upon your unique situation. "Being between projects," is how author Eric Butterworth, in his book *Spiritual Economics*, referred to unemployment and career transition. I loved the positive concept of these words that clearly stated the truth, "I am between projects." This was a hopeful way to answer the common question, "What do you do for a living?"

With this new perception, you can have a level of comfort in social situations, rather than declining and shying away from them. This also provides opportunity for those you are engaged in conversation with, to ask about your career experience and the projects you've participated in. You never know, you could get a referral and be working on a project or be in an interview the following day as a result of your communication. What a lovely way to honor yourself by stating positively, "I am between projects," rather than the statement that perpetuates the condition: "I am unemployed"; "I was laid off"; "I am a victim of corporate restructuring or downsizing." Remember the question, "Based on results, how can I have the same thoughts, attitudes, behaviors, and beliefs about a career crisis, career transition, or career change and expect a different result?"

As we take on each role in life, we assume an identity to perform the role. When the role changes, quite obviously our identity is also in for a shift. Perhaps a complete breakaway from the role is in divine order. Thankfully, there are organizations and associations that assist people with awareness regarding employment. One of the times I was between projects, I was referred to a career futures program. In the first week we went through a comprehensive series of human resource-related documents. At the end of the week I created a profile of the tabulated results and this was then input to a choices computer program. At the conclusion of this exercise the computer presented me with a list of the careers/jobs I'd be best suited for, based on the data I'd collected throughout the week. My list had seventeen entries on it, nine of which I had already done. This was encouraging and affirming of the accuracy of this valuable self-directed aspect of the program.

Quite a departure from my past habit of taking the first available job that came up simply to earn an income. It had been recommended by my healthcare professional that I make a career change. So, I gave myself the gift of the time to make a decision that would allow me to create a balanced lifestyle rather than simply do a job to create an income. This was certainly a breakaway from my conventional thinking, acting, behaving, and believing. I did not want to work just to pay the bills. I wanted to create a life-giving, rewarding career. During my decision-making and transition stage, I did voluntary work in five of the eight remaining options and realized that, by investing less than one hundred hours in this way, these choices were not a fit for me at present. I did choose a new career, which afforded me more free time so I could wean myself off the workaholic habit and invest more time in recreation, in renewing my relationships, rejuvenating my soul, and practicing self-care and balance.

Perhaps a career change for you may involve pooling your time and talent in a job-share, or it may involve new education and training. Perhaps early retirement from the corporate domain is the best option for you, and you feel fulfilled doing voluntary service. Perhaps you decide to apply to an entrepreneur program to bring your ideas to life and be your own boss. Speaking of being your own boss, I know a soul who is such an awesome example of creating her own career. She is an inspiration, who chooses to generate a full-time income by doing three distinctly differ-ent jobs that she is passionate about, each on a part-time basis. You may choose this option.

I would like to tell you that although I have made career changes in my life by choice, I have been laid off, fired, and unemployed as well (I mean between projects). I have expe-rienced living on employment insurance benefits and guar-anteed available income for need (welfare). I did identify that my weakest link was marketing myself. Thankfully, there were community-based programs to assist me to learn how to effectively market myself. Each time I was between projects, the time-frame lessened. I very clearly remember the range of my emotions – shock, anger, grief, feeling hopeless, and being in the pit of despair wanting to end it all at one end of the spectrum, to affirmative prayer at the other.

The last time I received a lay-off notice from work, I told a group of friends. At the end of the evening, before this individual left to go home, she said she felt compelled to pray with me. I cannot tell you a word of what she said; I just know that it was a very powerful experience. I cried myself to sleep that evening and upon rising I was blessed with this positive affirmation: "Thank you, God, that I receive confir-mation of my new full-time career before _____ [I filled in the date of my last day of work before lay-off] as _____ [I filled in the title of the position I had been applying for] or something better for the highest good of all."

Each time my mind would go to work with fear and anxiety over losing my job, I would endeavor to silently make this affirmation. Believe me, it was a tug of war, with my mind wanting to disasterize: "Oh, I'm gonna end up on welfare again." However, I was not at the mercy of these thoughts and did not allow them to sabotage me and to birth days of despondency and depression. That was the old way I had dealt with things. I had an opportunity to think new thoughts and create a new experience. Consequently, after a few interviews and within ten days of receiving my thirty-day lay-off notice, I was offered and accepted a new job.

I understand that although some of us have had occasion to leave one job on a Friday and begin a new job the following Monday, there are many of us who have experienced being between projects for years as we rehabilitated following illness, injury, divorce, and many other real-life experiences that complicate our lives.

There are limitless possibilities and all that is required is for you to change how you think, act, behave, and believe with regard to career. Thankfully, you are not alone, and help is available to you in a myriad of forms. Unlike past generations where people had one career for their entire lives, on average you may experience five to seven or more career changes in your lifetime.

Breakaway analogy in relationships example

Let's explore breakaway experience with regard to crises in

a relationship, and this includes your relationship with yourself. Despondency, depression, isolation, paranoia, fear, chaos, adulterous affairs, confusion, lackluster living on automatic pilot, may all reflect a crisis in the relationship or a lack of relationship with self. On my hike of my life adventure, I was presented with a time to face my reality, which meant that I had to stop denying and resisting my inner misery. I was finally ready to tell myself the truth and shine my inner light into the secret cave of my private pain. In public, I always had a smile on my face. I even purchased smiley-face self-inking stamps. I used them for years on notes, letters, and cards in my personal and professional life. I even had smiley-face earrings and I wore clothes that had the smiley-face symbol etched into the fabric. I had learned very young in life that people liked being in the company of those who were smiling. I learned that when I was in other, less amicable, moods and I was often separated from present company and isolated. I managed to put on a happy face for years.

For a good portion of my adult life, when in social or business situations, it was a medicated or numbed smile from the overindulgence of food, alcohol, or drugs. I could tell jokes too, not that I would want to share any of them now. However, I could go on for hours and have everyone laughing so hard that their faces and bellies hurt. This was a clever, yet empty, disguise, which distracted me from telling myself the truth about how I was really feeling. I had shut myself down emotionally. My strategy had worked for years. I made sure I had a very busy and full calendar that left no time to feel.

Exercise

Do you know who you really are? Do you have any idea of what you need and want? Do you know what makes you tick? Do you even like yourself, let alone love yourself?

When I asked myself these questions it sparked an internal revolution and quest of self-discovery. When the emotional aspect wants conscious acknowledgment, I would recommend listening to the little nudges, rather than waiting for the emotional breakdown. Can you relax without going out to be with someone, without doing something, or without taking something? Can you just sit still and be with yourself?

Based on results, how can I continue to have the same thoughts, attitudes, behavior, and beliefs about myself and expect a different result in my relationship with self? Is it time to interview a couple of counselors, personal coaches, spiritual advisors, psychologists, or an individual who has adequate life experience in all areas? Is it appropriate for you to investigate some human awareness and self-study development courses? Only you know what is best for you. However, a truth I adopted from a course I took was, "The degree to which I know and understand myself is equal to the degree my life works." Yes, you can create a life-giving, loving relationship with yourself and perhaps experience greater degrees of inner peace and fulfillment!

Personal example

I know when, in my journey of self-discovery, I have learned that my life relationship challenges and beliefs affect all my relationships, which for me is inclusive of the one I have with the God of my understanding, with myself, and with all others. Here is an example to demonstrate this last statement.

While attending a weekend retreat we were invited to do an exercise with regard to life relationship challenges. What came up for me was staggering and when I released the limiting root core belief, it was transformational. In my head I intellectually knew that others have done their best with regard to my socialization, schooling, and upbringing. However, in my heart I believed that it was just not good enough. I guess this was because every time I made a mistake it was brought to my attention. I was punished or reprimanded and at times I was humiliated when my errors were made public. In my head, I acknowledge that everyone does the best they know how to do, given their level of skill and ability at the time. In my heart I withheld love because they were not worthy. They did not deserve love for they had not earned love. This I had learned in relationships with others.

There was more that contributed to my belief in, and practice of, conditional love. When I was introduced to God in my very young years, I was introduced to a judgmental, punitive God. I related to God in the same way I described in the aforementioned paragraph. In my head I knew that God loved me, but in my heart I did not allow the love in, because I did not believe I was worthy of it, I did not deserve it, because I had not earned it. Can you see how this belief system has infected my relationship with myself, by creating and perpetuating low self-esteem, and my inability to accept self-love? I must admit to you that there have been times in my life when I was invested in self-hate. Can you see how this belief system has inhibited my personal relationship with the creator of all that is seen and unseen? Can you see how this belief system has robbed me of the joy of life-giving loving relationships?

This, thankfully, was learned and consequently I can willingly surrender this limiting belief and ask for miraculous healing and transformation of this thought energy. The incredible surprise came when I surrendered this in prayer and asked for divine assistance – I experienced a miracle in my self-worth, which now ripples through me and out to all, for the highest good of all. I could never have written and released this book had this not happened, because I would not have believed it was good enough. This good enough brand of conditional love has been passed from generation to generation.

In my experience, conditional love and manipulation are siblings. Both stipulate that if you behave in a certain way you are rewarded. If you study and earn high grades, you are recognized and approved of. If you pray and attend this type of house of worship, you are acceptable in God's eyes. If you support this political affiliation, play this sport, have this partner, drive this car, live in this neighborhood, speak this language, are a member of this gang or club – the list is endless – then you are worthy of my love. Conditional love is a hook. I will love, approve of, accept you only if this or that condition is met. If you love me the way I expect you to love me, then I'll love you. If you don't, then I will withhold or withdraw love until you conform and meet my condition. The extremes of conditional love then evolve into: drop you, ignore you, condemn you, and even hate you, just because you did not meet my conditional expectation.

Is it time to breakaway from conditional love and all of its malignancies that infect our global family? The practice of unconditional love begins as an inside job. It is a valuable process to identify the learned conditions, and recognizing the barriers within self to the belief in and practice of unconditional love. One aspect of the process is to free ourselves first by forgiving and accepting our own humanness.

No one handed us a playbook that detailed the game plan for our lives. If we're breathing, we're living and if we're living, we're learning. Of course, we're going to make mistakes. It's by acknowledging our mistakes truthfully, freeing ourselves from the destructive consequences of keeping secrets, that we learn unconditional love. Symptoms of giving us the gift of unconditional love are compassion, understanding, empathy, acceptance, appreciation, gratitude, patience, and kindness. Each day I can take responsibility and check in with myself by asking, "How did I love today?"

Love energy is very subtle, palpable, and powerful. I am confident that you can scan your life and come forward with significant examples of your personal experience of unconditional love. Love energy is to be shared. It is so simple. Love energy moving through each heart, filling the wholeness of each being, and flowing through interpersonal interactions, is unconditional love in action.

The complicated part for each of us is to identify the limiting thoughts, attitudes, behaviors, and beliefs about conditional love. Then free self bit by bit from these blocks to the experience of the full cycle of unconditional love energy. Does it happen overnight? Hardly, it is a life-giving practice of unconditional love for self first and then it naturally flows through you unimpeded.

Breakaway analogy in a personal lifestyle change example

Another breakaway example with regard to change of lifestyle which definitely affects our relationships. I experienced new and different friends when my marriage partner and I freed each other to go our separate ways. Married folks in my experience, with the exception of a few noble friends, exclude single people when entertaining because they hang out with couples. Also, as you make positive lifestyle changes you will find that some of the people with whom you choose to associate also change.

When I decided to clean up my act and make healthier choices, my relationships changed. In my drinking, drugging, smoking days I had entirely different places that I frequented for entertainment, and in some cases the folks I associated with are no longer in my life. Once I gave up the use of these substances, I invested in other pursuits and interests and consequently met like-minded people.

"All or nothing"

I spoke earlier about a retreat weekend, where one exercise we were asked to do was to make a list of five key relationships now and five key relationships of our lives. There was another limiting belief that had woven a destructive pattern throughout my life, which emerged from my asking, "What is a challenge I need to be aware of in my key life relationships?" A second one came up for me. I had a limiting belief that I had adopted in my very young years, which was demonstrated to me over and over again. This was the "all or nothing" attitude. I had witnessed when there were difficulties in relationships, where there was no being seen, heard, acknowledged, or validated to air the difference of opinion or perception. No opportunity to brainstorm together for all possible solutions, and no opportunity to choose together the best win/win option for the highest good of all. There was no opportunity to make sense of the challenge as a problem to be resolved or at least compromised. Over and over again, I saw that when there was a disagreement, these people were no longer in our lives.

Have you experienced any drama and/or trauma of "all or nothing" in your life? Is there an estranged friend, co-worker, classmate, business partner, coach, brother, sister, niece, nephew, uncle, aunt, parent, that you desire to reconnect with?

Personal story

During a course I was taking, the participants were given a homework assignment. We were requested to complete an incomplete communication. I chose an uncle I had not seen for some twenty-seven years. I made a visit to the hospital he was in and as I was going to the veteran wing I walked right into the path of my ex-sister-in-law. I was so shocked when she said in an angry voice, "What are you doing here?" I just sat down and wept. When I was able to speak again, I informed her that I was en route to visit my uncle whom she had never met. So I was provided with opportunity to complete two incomplete communications in one go. I did visit each of them more than that one time.

Is it time to breakaway from this destructive cycle of "all or nothing" in your life? What is true about me is that there is a wake of broken relationships and friendships behind me. The amazing thing for me was when I finally took responsibility for my adherence to this limiting belief and surrendered it to Spirit for healing and transformation – it was miraculous. It was also very freeing to tell myself the microscopic truth about how this "all or nothing" attitude had wreaked havoc in many other areas of my life, not just in relationships.

"All or nothing" attitude and the effect it has on decision – making

On one occasion I desired to purchase a laptop computer. I priced out brand new equipment with the programs that I wanted and then spent months moping about borrowing computers because I could not afford to buy what I wanted. It wasn't until later that I became conscious of my "all or nothing" attitude and how it had deterred me from getting a computer, period. Within days of my "ah-ha" realization, I purchased a used laptop computer from a reliable source, which gave the same warranty on a used purchase that is provided with new purchases.

The wonder-filled gifts that have evolved from my choice to surrender this limited way of living are too numerous to mention. However, some of the best were reconnection, reunion, and reconciliation with dear souls I truly do care about and hadn't seen for a long time. In one case thirty-four years had passed, in others twenty-five years, fourteen years, and in others five or six years. We can never regain lost time, and there will always be a gap of the years we missed. Thankfully, we did reconnect. Some are committed to sharing and supporting each other, while the purpose of reconnection with others was closure. It truly is a miracle to experience both ends of the spectrum with regard to "all or nothing" in relationships and then commit to learn how to effect a wholesome balance.

Breakaway from no boundaries to setting clear boundaries in relationships with regard to support

Part of the learning to effect a wholesome balance in rela-tionship with others is to set clear support boundaries with friends, colleagues, relatives, counselors, teachers, spiritual communities, mentors, advisors, and healthcare profession-als. In order to set clear boundaries with respect to support, first you need to define it. What is support? How can I support myself? How can I support others? What does a sup-portive environment look like? What does support in friend-ship feel like? Do I differentiate in the support I experience with regard to friendship, co-worker, or relative? How can I possibly support someone else until I learn to be supportive of myself?

I learned very quickly that others do not necessarily want to be supported in the same way I do, or in the way I think they ought to be supported. The consequence of pro-viding support to someone who did not enter into an agree-ment with me with regards to support, or ask for support, has been extremely educational. I learned that when I knock on a door that is closed, all I do is make noise and get sore knuckles. That is a comical way of saying, "Ask before you offer support because the reaction to unsolicited support is not at all pleasant. Wait for the open door to come to you." Individuals naturally resist change, get defensive, justify their actions, and a symptom of this is, when they are not ready for change, they exert force and push away the stimulus. When it appears on the surface that they are pushing you away, they are actually pushing away the energy flowing through you (the ideas or perceptions). Perhaps this is because they simply desire to be seen, heard, acknowledged, and validated. They do not want you to attempt to fix their problem, propose ideas or resolve their issues for them. In my experience, when I offered unsolicited support to someone, each of the ideas that I offered would be promptly followed by an excuse or reason why it wouldn't work. This is how I concluded that I was giving support in a manner that was not in fact supportive to the needs of the individual to whom I offered the support.

Based on results, I made appropriate changes when I approached the subject of support by asking the following questions. How can I support you? Can I pray for you or with you? Do you desire the gift of listening? Do you need resource referrals? Do you want to brainstorm for some ideas about your issue? Do you wish to borrow some books or cassettes? Do you need to be embraced and held in silence, so you can simply know you are not alone? Do you need a ride to take a course? Do you need some meals prepared while you recover from surgery? Do you want emotional support through a crisis? Do you wish me to encourage your creative endeavor? Do you wish me to partner with you in progress for your desired healthy action plan? May I spend quality time getting to know your children so you have some time to yourself? Do you want support in person, over the phone, in the mail, handwritten, or e-mail at the present time? What does support look like to you? How do you wish to be supported?

This new constructive approach to support is certainly a breakaway from the destructive habitual co-dependent conditional, enabling, controlling, and "all or nothing" relationship patterns. Thank goodness that change is possible. May I point out that you need to be willing to be clumsy while you're learning new skills. It is so important to be compassionate with yourself and each other in relationship interactions. Endeavor to be understanding and ask yourself, "What would love do here?"

When we are learning to ask for, give, and receive support, we will not be in synch all the time. I have had personal experience of times when I needed support while a dear soul in my life was learning to say "No." I had taken it personally, until I learned the facts by listening to what was going on in the life of the other person at the time of my request for support. This presented me with plenty of opportunities to address my controlling and self-centered attitude in relationships with others and replace it with understanding. The beauty of being dedicated to lifelong learning is that I acknowledge that we are all works in progress – "under construction," so to speak – and this provides heaps of space for leniency. When I experience understanding and leniency first-hand, then I am able to offer the same to others in the form of compassion.

Breakaway with regard to death, dying, and grieving

When a significant other is no longer a participant in your life, you can liken it to the passage through a turbulent storm when you look at grief solely from the personality perspective. The grief process, whether the breakaway relationship is death or divorce, can be weathered by honoring your emotions and not abandoning yourself in your time of need. Denial, anger, grief, despair, numbness, aloneness are the waves that carry us to new relationships with self and others.

In time we can give thanks and be grateful for the gift of the presence of the individual, realizing that some souls are with us for a reason, some for a season and some for a lifetime. In the made-for-TV movie produced by Oprah Winfrey, *Tuesdays With Morrie*, the character portrayed by Jack Lemmon said, "Death ends a life, not a relationship." The transition from life on earth, to life after life, is a change in form. Recently someone spoke of the topic of death with this quote: "Death is a cosmic change of address." To entertain these notions means a breakaway from a paradigm of thought and an opening up to a new soul perception of grief and death.

In the first couple of decades of my life, when someone died I was emotionally distraught and felt as though I had been catapulted into an abyss. In the last couple of decades, my experience has been very different. First, I do want to say that I was unable to talk about death with a dear soul and it was so difficult to watch him deteriorate and lose him to a disease. It was also very frustrating to feel helpless. A part of me knew, two weeks before this dear soul made his transition, that he was going to die. I cried and cried. When he did pass, I was able to function and help with all the details. We made a wall mural of memorabilia from his life with a banner that read: "Celebration of Life." This mural of photographs of the people with whom he chose to share his life became the focus of the get-together that followed the service. The mural proved what Burgess Meredith said in the movie *Grumpy Old Men*: "All we have are the experiences - the experiences!" I wore white to the service, because I was celebrating in my heart the transition of this dear soul. I knew he would not have to suffer any more here in the physical. In planning the service we selected the most positive uplifting readings we could find within the accepted traditional service. Of course, I missed the physical presence of this dear soul, but I have felt his spiritual presence around me. Frequently, in meditation and prayer time, I see him behind my closed eyes and ask that he receive blessings upon blessings in life after life, and I give thanks for the gift of his presence in my life.

Years later, when a dear soul I know was living with cancer, we talked about death and dying. Before this, I had feared my own mortality and could not talk about death. The truth is, we are all terminal; it is just a matter of when and how we will make our transition, not if we will make one.

I was unable to do this with others that I knew up until now. Spending time with her before she made her transition was very healing for me. I was able to tell her how much I loved her and appreciated all that we had shared together. I was able to tell her that each time I saw her I wondered if it would be the last. When I left to go around the world we agreed to meditate at a particular time on a particular day each month. I remember settling into accommodation in New Delhi, India, and I received the prompting that it was time to share a meditation experience with this dear soul at home, in the hospital in Canada. We had a wonderful shared meditation experience and I journalized a poem and we had a good laugh and a cry together.

Ten days later I made a note in my journal I had had an

exceptionally weepy day. Some time later, I received word through a mutual friend that she was no longer living with cancer and she had made her transition. I inquired regarding the date of her passing and I confirmed this as the day when I was particularly weepy over a month earlier. As I made my pilgrimage around the world, there were numerous occasions when I had dear friends come into my meditations to say goodbye. In a few instances when they were making their transitions, they would be on my mind so strong that I would sit to write them a letter of gratitude and thanksgiving. I posted the letter and in each case, the family told me when I returned after my pilgrimage that the one I had addressed the letter to died without getting a chance to read the letter, and the date I had written on the letter was the date they had made their transition. They did not receive and read the letter in its physical form, they received the energy of my thoughts directly.

When someone comes into your mind and they live a distance from you, honor it. They are thinking about you, they may be calling to you because they need help, they may wish to say goodbye before they make their transition. You have an innate ability to perceive subtle energy. Trust yourself when you receive the stimulation, and honor it.

Personal example

One soul I know telepathically called me to come and support his family and assist him in making his transition. He did not physically pick up the telephone and call me, we never spoke at all. A number of days in a row he appeared to me behind my closed eyes during my morning meditation. I called his stepdaughter and announced that I felt compelled to go see him and it had to be this coming weekend. She said she would accompany me on the journey, which would take a number of hours.

When we arrived at the hospital his breathing was labored and he was very anxious. At one point while I was holding his hand, he opened his eyes and raised his eyebrows in acknowledgment. He was unable to speak, as he had a huge tumor in his throat. I began to sing and hum a traditional hymn to him: "Be not afraid, I go before you always, come follow me and I will give you rest." Within minutes his breathing relaxed, as he did, and he was able to rest. His estranged son arrived to see him, and we both stood holding his hands, one of us on either side of the bed. While still holding our hands, the patient sat right up in bed with his eyes open and focused, and his arms stretched out and up toward the ceiling. I realized he was going toward the light, but had not yet figured out that he had to leave his physical body behind and make his transition in his energy/light/spiritual body. I knew at this point that he would soon make his transition, simply because another friend had described similar experiences when her husband and son were about to make their transitions.

The estranged son was preparing to leave the hospital and said he would come back the following weekend. I recommended that he stay a bit longer and we would give him privacy so that he could say his goodbye, because I believed his father would not be alive by the next weekend. I also suggested the rest of the family make time for their final shared moments. I held his wife's hand and encouraged her to tell him that she blesses him and lets him go. She assured her beloved that she would be okay, that he could go and not worry about her. He made his transition peacefully the next day. When we entered his hospital room, the sheet was up and over his head. We lifted the sheet to kiss him goodbye and his mouth was open from when he took his final breath. We replaced the sheet over his head. We held him and prayed. We moved down to the end of the bed and sat holding his feet until his wife was ready to leave. I saw the sheet move when we were sitting at the foot of his bed. When the others left the room, I went up and looked under the sheet at his face and this time his mouth was closed and he was smiling.

Another example

I was blessed with the inspiration to honor the memory of another dear soul when she made her transition after ninety-two years of life. Part of my grief process was to write in my journal a fond memory or funny story for each of her ninety-two years of age. A wonder-filled healing process was for me to laugh and cry as I made the list. One week before this individual had passed away, I felt her presence very strongly when I was in my kitchen. She shared the day with me as I prepared meals for the upcoming week. In my very young years, that was how I remembered her, always in the kitchen cooking and baking with her apron on, and the splendid privilege of sampling her cooking through numerous bites, licks, and tastes.

Another breakaway example

I would like to share a story I heard about two brothers who went to the lumberyard and purchased the finest wood they could find. They then spent the evening building their father's coffin. They also went to the graveyard and dug the grave themselves. In their opinion, too often we hire others to do these things for us. They considered it a privilege to do this for their dad. It also allowed them to really feel the pain of their loss and the depth of their sorrow as well as the great joy of having been loved by their dad. They claimed they could not have experienced one without the other. They were also very mindful and grateful for all they had shared with their dad.

Last example

I heard a story about a minister who was consoling some high-school students, the day of the death of one of their schoolmates. He gathered them into a circle and as they stood together on the lawn holding hands, he invited them to send light and love energy to the dearly departed and to his family. He also said that grief is healthy and healing at the same time. He explained to the youth that they would not be able to feel the pain, the sorrow, the grief of the loss of their schoolmate, if they had not been able to feel the joy, the happiness, and the love of having known him. This type of process leaps all restrictive boundaries placed upon us by traditions and is very life-giving and respectful.

Grief exercise

A grief exercise you may wish to do is to make a list of cherished memories of the one you held so dear. Recall the connections and embrace this therapeutic notion and create a list of fond memories, your personal appreciation of the gift of the presence of your beloved and your gratitude for what you shared in this life. If your interaction was short, I invite you to remember one for each day, month, or year your beloved was with you. This process is a wonder-filled way to honor your soul connection. We touch each other in unique ways in our shared life experiences, and giving thanks for the gift of the presence of a beloved soul is optimum reverence. When we attend memorial services or funeral receptions we can share our personal interaction stories and bless each other. In the process we all come to know and understand more of their whole life experience and not simply the way we knew them.

Jack Lemmon's character in the movie *Tuesdays With Morrie* had a living funeral so he could be present to hear all the lovely things that folks had to say about him. Then there are those who are living with cancer and chronic conditions that have video or tape-recorded messages prepared to give to those they will leave behind. What an inspiring concept, truly a breakaway from the traditional memorial service. We may even choose to provide our own tape-recorded or videotaped eulogy.

I know you have been given plenty to ponder and work with in respect of breakaway. When you're ready to leave this breakaway beach, close your eyes and visualize yourself turning away from the breakaway sandstone monolith and see yourself walking north on the sandy beach, along the shoreline of the ocean. Stroll and listen to the waves slapping rhythmically on the shore. Take in a few long, slow inhalations of the refreshing sea air. Feel the caress of the cool breeze against your flesh and notice how relaxed you are. Pause and face the ocean and in this serene nourishing environment, tune into your heart…

Tune into your heart

Your heart is divine connection to Spirit,
Be still and listen in order to hear it.
Build rapport relationship with your own heart,
To learn your passion, your purpose, your part.

Tune into your heart. Tune into your heart.
Tune into your heart and listen…

Rapport relationship with your own heart,
Provides the energy and courage to start.
You are a being of radiant light,
So rare, unique, and bright.

Tune into your heart. Tune into your heart.
Tune into your heart and listen…
You are rare, unique, pure light.

Cave Experiences

There you are, standing on the beach facing the ocean. Turn yourself so that your back is to the ocean and open your eyes. Ahead of you in the distance you see a huge inland crevice. You are curious and wish to explore this remarkable change in the landscape in this new ecosystem. As you make your way in that direction you are surprised and cannot believe the spectacular seashells embedded in rich, red earth walls that line the pathway. Is it possible that this entire mass of land was at one time under the ocean? How else would it be possible for the seashells to be embedded up so high? You continue on your way, and flanking the path stretched out before you are a collection of delicate green trees. This is such a dramatic contrast against the colored landscape. What is also interesting is how dry it is and how the dust from the red earth clings to the exposed bits of your socks. You'd expect being so close to the sea that it would be moist; however, this is not the case. Stretching out in front of you is a path that leads you to the entrance of a cave.

Imagination exercise

You stand at the entrance of the cave, focus your attention upon your heart and breath. You feel calm with each inhalation of the vital life-force even though your mind and heart are racing with anticipation and intrigue. Continue to breathe into your heart. You are conscious in this present moment experience and feel the life-force beating your heart, the beat of life. You breathe into your heart repeatedly and remind yourself of your limitless inner light. You shine it brightly, and say silently to yourself, "Go ahead and prepare the way for the highest good of all."

Know that your inner guidance is like a wise, intuitive owl. You will be led in a way of ease, in the most gentle, compatible way possible, so that you learn what you truly desire to learn. You can feel, deal and heal your past cave experiences by revealing the truth to yourself.

This is a new process of acknowledging that you are simply human, accepting your experience of life, rather than repeating the old habit of running away or hiding from the truth of your real-life experiences. An opportunity to use rather than conserve your courage. A choice to move through the various stages, from being a victim of what life has dealt you to being a survivor of the experience, and then thriving in your life free from the habit of keeping your past a secret from yourself and others. You are evolving in order to create the life you say is most important to you. You have all you need within you to go in and through the cave experience.

In this discussion using the analogy of a cave experience, although I realize that cave experiences vary as individuals vary, it is my intent that you will blaze a trail into each of your cave experiences with hope, knowing you are not the only one on earth to experience a cave. Shine your radiant inner light into each of your cave experiences, accepting your humanity and realizing our interconnectedness, the similarity of experience and our interdependence.

Take a few long, slow inhalations and exhalations, remembering the power in the very breath of life. Abundant breath, abundant heartbeats, abundant life, and abundant light flows from your heart-centre into the cave as you enter. It feels cool at first and you proceed slowly as the beam streaming from your heart lights the way. The trail is wide and the way is safe. It's amazing how quiet it is and how clear is the view.

The cave of abuse

Many of the dear souls upon the planet have passed through the vibration of experience known as abuse. Physical, emotional, sexual, psychological, racial discrimination, the ravages of war, or ritual abuse. In some cases, the nightmarish real-life events were so harsh and intense that the wounded aspect of self buries the memory in the depths of the subconscious. Each time an outer interaction or circumstance triggers the memory, it is unconsciously pushed away with "busy-ness," or we medicate or numb the self through drugs and/or alcohol, or other addictions like sex, gambling, overwork, shopping, shoplifting, job- or relationship-hopping, sports, caffeine, nicotine, or food.

There is an idiom I've heard many times, you may recognize it: "Time will heal, it's the past, forget it." And if you're like myself, I did forget it. For over three decades I had no conscious memory. However, the pain I experienced in my self-destructive habits was what transpired as a result of hiding from my hurts rather than healing them. Like many, I was taught to keep secrets, conceal the truth, and even conceal the crime. You may have heard the expression, "Don't air your dirty laundry in public." I certainly took that to heart, because I didn't air it at all, not even to myself. I encourage you to spend time and nurture and listen to your wounded aspect of self if, or when, it comes forward to you in the cave.

The techniques in the lush field of life section of this book may assist you. Then again, you may choose to interview some counselors so that you are not alone with your abuse-healing journey experience.

During my hike of my life adventure, I identified that I had developed neuroses to keep myself preoccupied in order for the wounded child aspect of self to feel safe in the outside world. I was driven to achieve and do. I was a human doing rather than a human being. For years I was a workaholic, driven to excel and perform so others were distracted from knowing my secrets. No time for intimacy in relationships because I spread myself so thin with so many interests and people. I invested plenty of energy being a perfectionist, leaving no room for criticism, mistake, or reprimand. I was so compulsive, obsessive, possessive, and competitive. Whenever I felt overwhelmed, I would retreat to fantasy and dream how life would be someday, because this is what I did to survive when the abuse was happening. I would energetically leave my body, because the experience was so heinous. "Life will be more pleasant when _____" was the belief I would cling to in order to feel better in the moment. My make-believe world kept me hoping that some day I'd do this or that and life would be better then. I was able to cope and survive under the deluge of my own compulsive shame thoughts and self-destructive behaviors. That was until I became willing to acknowledge and shine my brilliant inner light into my abuse cave experience.

This only happened when I was exhausted from attempting to run away from myself and when my acting-out behaviors and destructive habits had driven away nearly everyone that was dear to me. Then I had the courage to stop and ask myself, "Why is it I want someone else to do for me what I'm not willing to do for myself? Why is it I want someone else to love me when I'm not willing to love myself? Is the key to making time and space for a miraculous transformation of my own life dependent upon my learning to accept, nurture, and love myself unconditionally?"

When my traumatized, wounded aspect of self came forward into the light of my conscious awareness from the dark crevices of the cave, what a relief. I made the decision to stop medicating and numbing myself in order to feel, deal, heal, and reveal the truth to myself. This process spanned a decade and it was gentle and progressive, and I was never given more than I could handle at any one time. Sure, there was emotional, mental, spiritual, physical, physiological, psychological turbulence as well as joy, merriment, and celebration with each new understanding, as I let go of an old limiting thought, attitude, behavior, or belief to birth something new. It was a psychic slaughter of everything I held to be true, to determine for myself, "Is this true for me now? Does this serve me now?" The hike of my life adventure continues to be an incremental process of transformation from shame- and fear-based self-loathing to self-loving based on compassion and understanding.

I was inspired by two quotations from Kahlil Gibran, a Lebanese poet: "The height of your joy is equal to the depth your sorrow has dug within you," and "One must pass through the inferno of their passions in order to overcome them." I now consider a passion anything I give energy to. When I give energy to it, it has life and I know I live passionately. What a revelation to consciously consider the passion I give to my thought system. Whether I choose to think positive life-giving thoughts or negative self-destructive thoughts, they have life energy and there are consequences as a result of my thoughts.

Are you willing to enter the cave and allow your wounded aspect of self to tell you the truth about what they actually experienced? This is a process of freeing yourself from being a prisoner of your past. The process involves identifying the strategies you employ in order to stay safe in volatile environments, to keep the peace, to be seen and not heard.

During my healing journey I uncovered the truth of so many root core beliefs and habit patterns that no longer served me. I realized how I denied feelings, abandoned myself, betrayed myself, and kept quiet in order to stay safe. I rejected my sexuality and femininity because of the shame, guilt, and pain of being sexually abused. In the process I released a limiting belief which I had adopted that said I did not deserve pleasure. I took responsibility for and changed my self-talk, which initially perpetuated the belief that I was used goods, forever tarnished, rather than one who had passed through the vibration of sexual abuse. I used to believe that sex was something taken from me rather than something I participated in. I was shocked to discover that I felt responsible for meeting the needs of men who were sexually aroused. I believed that I was responsible when a man became stimulated, and obliged to comply. I thought my femininity was a curse and a cross to bear, rather than a gift I am free to express. The lie I learned from society at large was that when a woman has a man in her life she will be safe, whereas the truth for my wounded child aspect of self was that men caused pain.

When I was unconsciously living, with these opposing beliefs running at the same time, I had to medicate and numb myself before I could allow myself to engage in physically intimate relations with a man, even when I was married. When the abuses happened, in the majority of cases it was in the dark, and consequently I was afraid of the dark for years. In my adult life, when it came to sexual encounters I became drunk and numbed myself beforehand, which was a destructive cycle that repeated itself for years. Also, it did not feel comfortable for me to engage in sexual activity unless it was dark. I was so disconnected from my body, that I was oblivious of how to constructively meet my needs for intimacy and tenderness.

Have you ever heard of the notion that some people come into our lives for a reason, a season, or a lifetime? I met an interesting man and over time our relationship blossomed from friends to lovers. At the beginning of one weekend we shared an incredible intimate exchange which I sabotaged by getting blind drunk. In this particular case, I realized that this dear soul had come into my life for a reason when he asked me why I got so drunk. No one had ever asked me that. The truth is, my out-of-control, acting-out behavior was so appalling that not many stuck around. It was the question that hit me like a stun gun. He wasn't going to leave and he sincerely wanted to know why. I sat bewildered and frightened to tell the truth. I had told the truth before of the teenage sexual abuse I had experienced and to people who did not know how to, or did not want to, deal with the topic or the issues. I do not blame them for abandoning me emotionally – they knew not how to handle the situation and that's okay. Then of course there were those in my life who did not want to believe that it had happened. I know from my own experience of denial that it served me well as a coping strategy to stay unconscious, so one does not have to deal with the things which one is not yet ready to deal with.

My day of reckoning had arrived through a dear soul brother and a simple question, "Why did you do that, drink so much?" My response was not detailed. However, I did say that I did not have many positive experiences with regard to expressing my sexuality and femininity without guilt, shame, and remorse. My conditioned, warped, root core belief was that my body was dirty and sexual pleasure was a sin. This one question and the open-hearted listening empowered me to turn the corner from alcoholism to sobriety. From medicating myself with alcohol and taking prescription painkiller medication to a willingness to be curious about the pain and the journey through it to freedom.

In my reading, research, and recovery work, I was blessed by another dear soul, when he loaned me the book *Waking the Tiger - Healing Trauma* by Peter A. Levine. This excerpt really touched me and assisted me to stop my rampant guilt thoughts toward myself for my drunken promiscuity from two decades ago: "Looking at this man's behaviors without knowing anything about his past, we might think he was mad. However, with a little history, we can see that his actions were a brilliant attempt to resolve a

deep emotional scar. His re-enactment took him to the very
edge, again and again, until he was finally able to free
himself from the overwhelming nightmare."

The recovery process for anyone who has passed
through the vibration of the experience of any type of abuse
will be unique. However, when we share our stories it is a
way to reach out to say that you're not alone. A way to touch
the outstretched hand within the heart of another and allow
a miraculous healing to happen. Is this not the purpose of
relationship – mutual growth?

Another excerpt from Levine's book puts this succinctly:
"In many so-called primitive cultures, the nature of this
man's emotional and spiritual injuries would be openly
acknowledged by the tribe. He would be encouraged to
share his pain. A healing ceremony would be performed in
the presence of the whole village. With the help of his
people, the man would re-unite with his lost spirit. After this
cleansing, in a joyous celebration, the man would be
welcomed back as a hero."

What a revelation for those of us on the myriad healing
paths of abuse recovery, to consider ourselves to be heroes,
rather than used, damaged, or forever tarnished. The inner
torment of branding myself "damaged goods" made it near
impossible for me to allow myself to receive pleasure. The
very thing I craved, tenderness, was also what my wounded
aspect of self feared the most. I had been betrayed by those
I knew and trusted when I was very young and the consequence of that was that for much of my adult life I did not
trust myself. That was until Dr. Sidra Stone, in a private
"voice dialogue session," helped me to consciously separate
the wounded aspect of self from my instinctive, intuitive,
wise aspect of self. This is just one of many examples of God

in action in my life, and of divine timing.

This particular event transpired just weeks before I was scheduled to leave on my two-year pilgrimage around the world with myself. During this profound session, I reconnected and gained conscious access to my intuition.

A voice dialogue session is a method of sitting opposite from a trained facilitator while they dialogue with the various aspects of the personality of the client. In the dialogue and questioning process the client becomes conscious of those unique characteristics and qualities of their psychology of selves within that are engaged in any particular session. Each time a new aspect expresses itself, the client moves. This means at times the client may sit, stand, lie down, go lean against the wall, or stand in the doorway in order to be comfortable in the expression of this unique self. At the end of the session, which is about an hour or so in length, the client stands behind or beside the practitioner, who gives a detailed summary of what transpired and what was discussed during the session. The technique enables the client to become conscious of the various expressions of self in the psychology of selves within the wholeness of their personality.

In my case, Sidra gave invitation to the instinctive aspect of self to dialogue with her. This part of me sat on the floor and was really grounded, present, and in tune with her surroundings and very attentive with Sidra. She spoke to this aspect and in the conversation that transpired reminded me of all the gifts and talents that are part of the natural expression of this aspect of self. At a pivotal point in my conversation with her, my eyes became tearful and she said, "Move." In that instant, my wounded child was separated from my intuitive wise owl aspect of self. My instinctual child, before my experience of abuse, was intact, keen, and wise. This explained why, in my adult life, I had been plagued with difficulty in trusting myself in new situations and in making decisions. This also explained why the doer, controller, pusher, perfectionist energies were so strong in me, because my instinct was not accessible to assist me with decisions. The dominant selves ran the show, so to speak, in order to keep me safe. The incredible gift of this particular session was that I was now consciously aware with clear access to my innate instinctual heritage that serves me well now and kept me safe while I journeyed to and through unfamiliar places around the world.

Dr. Sidra Stone also explained the natural process of all youngsters as their bodies mature. She stated that about age five for girls and a little later for boys, children began to become aware of their sexuality. She went on to say that it is normal innocent curiosity for children to want to discover the difference in body design between boys and girls. When playing youngsters frequently lift up their cloths and touch themselves. They delight acknowledging new sensitivities from the stimulation.

For me to hear this was such a relief. Initially, I had acted upon a genuine innocent curiosity when I engaged in a discovering of each other process with a genuine innocent little boy. However, when those older than I took advantage of my innocent curiosity for their own gratification a terrible ordeal evolved. My innocence was repeatedly abused.

Chances are, I am not the only one to have experienced these types of circumstances. It became obvious to me that sexuality can be a very complicated issue. Especially when the adult me yearns to experience a life-giving loving intimate relationship, but, the wounded child burdened with un-healed sexuality issues inhibits this realiszation. Thankfully, there are specialists to assist, so it is possible to work through and heal these unresolved past issues when and if it feels appropriate.

Before continuing I feel compelled to say this:

> "I am so sorry for the abuse you may have endured. I am so sorry it happened to you. I hope it comforts you to know you are not the only one to have had this experience."

My whole life I waited for an apology, and finally me the adult gave it to me the wounded child. Then I could move on and gradually feel, deal and heal this complicated part of my past. I hope it comforts you to know you are not alone, and you do not have to keep it all a secret any longer.

I must admit, I was very resistant to come back home after my world pilgrimage. During the profound voice dialogue session I agreed to let my wounded aspect rest while I practiced expressing my instinctive energy. I knew upon returning home that I had to allow more time for the wounded aspect of my self to feel, deal, and heal. It was a whole new season of counseling, support groups, art therapy, and more. I realized I was emotionally stunted and, although an adult, I operated from an emotional kinder-garten at times. As an adult dealing with situations as they occur, when I reacted I knew it was because I gauged the present using a warped emotional meter of my wounded self from the past. I now know this was the very process that would assist me in dealing effectively with my emotions, by first honoring them and learning new methods of managing them. Emotional self-management is truly a gift we give ourselves, and then each other, because in the process we experience a "care with passion" brand of compassion.

A woman I know was invited to an audience with the Dalai Lama. She had brought a gift to give to his Holiness but did not have it with her because her luggage had been lost. When it came to her turn in the processions to go up and have a one-to-one moment with him, she held out her hands, palms up, and said, "I give my heart." The Dalai Lama responded, "Fill with compassion." I give thanks that she related this story – it is a message each of us can choose to learn to put into practice. What a difference we will make in our own life and in the lives of all with whom we interact. Love is the most powerful force and source of healing energy in the world and compassion is an aspect of loving well. We are learning and practicing through the lens of our lives in relationships with others, how to love and love well.

For a short season in my life I was involved with a married man. We met in secret and both of us were meeting some needs, albeit destructively. In my healing journey I finally realized I deserved more. I was worthy of more than a measly six hours a month. I finally thought myself worthy to create a life-giving intimate relationship with an emotionally available man. I had been unconsciously living the pattern created over three decades earlier in my experience of sexual abuse. Here was a present-day re-enactment to bring me to the edge, to heal a deep emotional scar and break the vicious cycle of abuse I was perpetuating in my own life. I became conscious of the similarities with the help of a trusted counselor. This relationship transpired in the dark (this secret affair), with the other individual totally in control of our meeting times, communication times, and the duration of our visits.

Learning to love myself unconditionally was and is part of the process. In time I was anchored in a new belief that I deserved more, and once I was clear I made the choice to break off the relationship. I asserted definite clear boundaries. I put strategies in place to meet my tenderness and touch needs in life-giving ways, beginning with massage and reflexology. Plus, I purchased a goose down duvet, more pillows and a flannel sheet set to snuggle into daily.

Also, I acknowledged how most of the men I had chosen for relationships were not at all emotionally available to me, nor had I been to myself. The biblical truth demonstrated this so succinctly for me: "As I sow, so also shall I reap."

I also learned that in the past, I had been attracted to men who were disciplined, secure, and financially stable. With the support of a counselor I realized that it was these qualities that I needed to develop and demonstrate in my own life.

While on the subject of truth...

Have you ever seen the American movie *The General's Daughter?* One Father's Day I was prompted to turn on the television to watch a movie and afterwards I wept for hours and journalized much. In the movie a woman in an evening army exercise was brutally tied up and repeatedly raped. Her father, an officer, was debriefed before he was permitted to visit his traumatized, battered, and bruised daughter in the hospital. In the movie his character was instructed by his superiors that this could not go public, that it would be best if he told his daughter that it didn't happen and never to speak of it to anyone, ever. Truth concealed and a crime concealed. My guess is that this is true for millions. There are millions who have been the victim of abuse or of a crime, or the witness to a crime or abuse as a child, adolescent, or even as an adult.

When the essence of who we are in truth is not honored by those about us, and when we are threatened with our lives, to keep silent sets up a destructive pattern, an unwillingness to tell the truth – "If I tell the truth, I'll be further abused, punished, and threatened." So in some cases, unconsciously, we continue living with our private pain to the best of our ability, concealing the truth to keep the peace externally but robbing ourselves of internal peace.

It was difficult, yet healing, to watch this movie and it certainly was not a coincidence. I needed to see this dramatization in order to give myself permission to tell myself the truth – the whole truth – and admit to myself that there were many in my life, for valid reasons at the time, who concealed the truth in an attempt to protect all concerned. Thankfully, I gifted myself with permission to break this cycle and stop denying the truth by concealing it. A gift from this new awareness and understanding was the opportunity to forgive myself and all others involved.

Forgiveness of self

Forgiveness of self is part of the path.
Soft, salty tears make a warm, cleansing bath.
Forgiveness of self is part of the path.
Surrender the chains, be free of the past.
Know peace, at last.

The perfectionist cave

My knowledge and understanding of the perfectionist cave, was that when a care-giver or a significant other punished me for making a mistake, I felt shamed. As a child, I was doing the best I knew how to do at the time, given my level of skill, knowledge, and ability. Each time the mistake, fault-finding, or acting-out behavior was dealt with, I, the individual, was punished, and at times publicly embarrassed and/or shamed. Over and over I had it pointed out to me in a toxic manner that reinforced the message: "I wasn't good enough." A part of me screamed in my head at one point when I, in a present moment event, triggered a past memory: "What's more important this _____ or me?" As a child, I did not know how to separate the scolding of the incident, the _____ [the material thing, the acting-out behavior], from the self. I had been repeatedly punished for my faults, errors, and mistakes. I had learned through this type of experience that I was bad, wrong, and I believed I was worthless. Had I heard "I love you no matter what" or had I heard "It is this acting-out behavior, this unskilled behavior, that is not acceptable," I would have learned to differentiate. Consequently, over time I came to believe that it was I who was unacceptable because the scolding, reprimands, and punishment were all heaped together. There was no distinction made between the precious soul that I am in truth, and the error. And so it is with you. You are a precious soul and that is the undeniable truth.

When I believed the limiting thought: "Even though I did my best, my best wasn't good enough," I learned to not appreciate, value, or honor the positive, because others rarely did. Thankfully, now I accept, approve of, and appreciate the good. However, up until now, I learned to focus on the negative. My conditioned belief and habit pattern was that I would point out shortcomings, find faults and mistakes, instead of giving gratitude and appreciation for all that was right. My learned habit of shame became one of self-condemnation and self-loathing. I was unable to look myself in the eye in the mirror without finding fault in my appearance. Much of the time my internal mental dialogue would focus on my mistakes, what I said or did wrong. Oh, how internally critical I had become. I had to admit that I had become a chronic nit-picker. At times I would speak out loud my criticism and harsh judgment of others, yet that did not hold a candle to the constant inner barrage of my toxic thoughts.

Another destructive habit I identified was that I would abandon and betray myself by not speaking up in the moment and then I would nurse, curse, and rehearse the scenario in my mind. This did not just happen once either. Whenever a similar situation came up I would nurse, curse, and rehearse the whole spectrum of events, and this would catapult me into another abyss of depression and beating myself up, which was a further betrayal of self.

Personal story as an example

I had a friend who lived abroad ring me up on the telephone to ask if she could come for a three-week visit, and at the time she offered to share living expenses. I agreed to the visit even though I was living in shared accommodation and between projects (not working for an income).

By the time my guest arrived I was working part-time,

had rented and moved into my own place, and purchased on credit a futon bed and a car. The visit proceeded and this individual did not keep her own agreement to share expenses and even requested to extend her stay from three to six weeks. I said it was okay, and this was when I abandoned myself by not speaking my truth in the moment. We were in the car, I was driving and we were en route to a function, and almost immediately after I responded with "yes," when I really did not want to, the car was rear-ended. Talk about a nudge from the universe to honor myself. I just wanted to keep the peace. I had these opposing beliefs running and consequently sabotaged my own happiness. Have you ever said yes when you wanted to say no?

My credit card debt was mounting, this individual did not keep her agreement to contribute financially, and I had to ask for money, which was a very unsettling experience for me. She expected me to be glad to have a visitor and to show her around. Under normal circumstances, with a full-time income, of course I would have been, as I have been numerous times. The convenience of having me as a driver, with a vehicle at our immediate disposal, and of all the hospitality, was expected of me and not appreciated. I did not have the courage at the time to discuss the entire situation before she continued on her trip, and there was a definite rift. This was the result of my inability to speak my truth, set clear boundaries, and resolve conflict.

The consequence of this was a vicious cycle of every other similar past circumstance coming up as I nursed, cursed, and rehearsed how I could have, should have, would have handled this present situation. A situation where to keep the peace I had concealed my truth. It took me quite some time to be grateful for what I learned from this experience and even longer until I was willing to surrender my unforgivingness toward myself and my house guest from abroad.

The cave of shame

Years ago, I had worked with some wonderful material by John Bradshaw entitled *Healing the Shame That Binds You.* In it he explained our cultural learned habit of the continuum of shame. He labeled the practice "toxic multi-generational shame." The effect of this type of shame is that one believes one is shame. At this juncture of the hike of my life adventure I was learning how destructively rampant this force was in my life. With new understanding from this book on cassette, I accepted and acknowledged the truth of all the external shaming in order to feel, deal, and heal and to set myself free from it. Yet I had skillfully denied my habit of self-shaming, self-loathing, and self-condemnation. That was, until I attended a shame workshop some eight years later.

I was desperate for answers because I was so depressed and nothing was working in my life. My health, my career, my relationships, and my finances were in shambles. I felt helpless and thought I was going crazy. I had a screaming, morbid, debilitating inner voice yelling: "I HATE MY LIFE, I WISH I WAS DEAD!" At this workshop I told the truth of what my inner voice had been screaming for a couple of months. I identified this as my inner voice of shame. The voice lost its power to control me when I admitted to myself and witnessed that the voice actually existed.

Then came the work of observing and catching myself

each time I thought a shaming thought about any incident in my life. I would say, "Shame, I know you. I recognize you. You are not in control of my life any more. The truth is that I am precious. I am rich. I am an uplifting force in society. I am miraculous new perception. I am healing. I am hope. I am solutions. I am grateful for life. I am synthesized. I am more than the sum total of everything I have thought, said, and done. I am more."

I made it a practice to admit to myself and write down each thought where I shamed myself by comparing myself to others or when I reprimanded myself for making a mistake or when I felt shamed by someone else. It took an incredible amount of discipline. This was the real practice of self-love, self-understanding, and filling my heart with compassion. The degree of peace I experienced as a result was well worth the diligent, determined, and persistent effort. A new, constructive, life-giving habit of accepting my humanness soon replaced the old destructive habit of shaming myself through self-condemnation. I learned how to say, "Oh, well – I am human. Things don't always turn out the way I or others expect them to, and that's okay. Living is about learning and I am dedicated to lifelong learning."

By the way, I do not use all of the tools and techniques I describe and discuss in this book at the same time. They are part of my supportive tool-chest that has evolved as a result of making my hike of my life adventure over the past two decades. It is great to have so many tools for personal transformation that I can pull out and use to effect a needed or desired change.

A shaming example

Here's a description of what I mean. I've had many opportunities to do house- and pet-sitting service. On one such
occasion, I had cleaned and made ready the interior and
exterior of the home and really put myself out. There were
many lessons in this series of circumstances. I was replaying
a life-pattern, being the pleaser in action, trying to earn
acceptance and approval from external sources. When they
arrived home over the next few days, every imperfection was
brought up. This catapulted me into the past when, through
shaming, I perpetuated a limiting belief that I was "damned
if I did and damned if I didn't." In victim mode, I became
resentful and went into days of nursing, cursing, and
rehearsing the past. Every other experience in which I had
felt the same way came rushing back to me and I was on a
negative spiral into another depression. After a few days I
cried out in frustration and wrote in my journal: "What is
the lesson I am to learn from this?"

I had to learn to give myself the acceptance, approval,
and appreciation that I had done my best and that my best
was good enough. I affirmed that I am a soul, and so
valuable compared to the value of _____. Whatever the
fault, mistake, acting-out behavior, broken or soiled
material possession, I cannot be replaced, but the material
things can be. This incident, which to some would appear to
be inconsequential, was the window of opportunity that
assisted me to grow beyond my limiting beliefs. Those
material things are not more valuable than my soul, and
mentally beating myself up about my error kept me stuck in
the "I'm not good enough" condition. I got it – that it was
my thinking and shaming myself that was causing my mental

anguish. Also, my fear of telling the truth taught me how afraid I was to admit my mistakes. In my self-study I remembered that in the past admitting mistakes and telling the truth had been an experience of pain, punishment, isolation, emotional abandonment, public humiliation, embarrassment, and, on one occasion, the fear of losing my life. My wounded aspect of self had learned early in life that the consequence of speaking up was in many cases severe and harsh. I learned that it was safer to keep quiet, and to keep a secret.

Exercise

In school, with the grading system that was in place, perfection was rewarded. We were disciplined and forcibly managed to conform, to learn, to earn grades, and we were all taught the same material. What a departure from receiving encouragement to be creative and receiving permission to express our unique gifts and talents. Perhaps not now, but in the past, students have been publicly punished for mistakes. Thankfully, today people are waking up to the notion that it is appropriate to separate the unskilled or acting-out behavior from the person. It is, after all, the behavior that is unacceptable and not the precious soul.

In the event that you make mistakes, try this positive, affirming dialogue with yourself: "_____ [fill in the blank with your name], I love you no matter what. I will never leave you, punish you, or abandon you. You are a beloved, precious soul and that is the truth. This acting-out or unskilled behavior can be changed, this material thing can be replaced, and you are divine and wonderful. Simply

92

because you exist, you are worthy – you need not earn love or positive regard from anyone, including yourself. Simply because you exist, you are worthy – there is no other requirement than this. I love you. You are the very essence of love itself."

This dialogue is a gift you give yourself. It is acceptance of your humanness. Using this tool, you can sequentially accept all of your life experiences as, when, and if you are ready to do so. All you have in life are your experiences. When you are in your moments of acknowledgment of your humanness, I encourage you to practice this type of dialogue: "Oops, my mistake. Oops, silly spill. Oops, broken plate. Oops, negative thought. Oops, handled that poorly, I know I'll do it differently next time." This is the type of dialogue you practice silently or aloud. The more you practice, the more conditioned it becomes, and this will become your natural response when in the company of others. The ripple effect of respect-filled, honoring, self-talk becomes compassionate and accepting language in the home, workplace, community, the nation, and our world.

Cave of religiosity

As a youngster, when I was instructed in religion, I was introduced to a judgmental, punitive God. What a heavy burden to place upon a young child, to live with the fear of death by condemnation and burning in hell. Thankfully, the learned notion of being a sinner heaped with guilt and shame can be unlearned. Now, it is no wonder the perfectionist is such a powerful, dominant aspect of self very early in life, especially in its attempts to keep the child safe from abuses of a physical, emotional, psychological, and spiritual nature.

There was an aspect of myself that knew that this depiction of a judgmental, punitive God was not true, and I struggled with this for many years. Thankfully, in my adult years of exploration I have had a totally new and different experience of the God of my understanding. One of the major gifts from my studies was in learning this interpretation of the meaning of the word religion. The word "religion" in its Latin root derivative is "religare." "Ligare" means to connect. Therefore, religion in truth is more accurately "religare," which means to reconnect.

What a relief for me to determine that all the world religions, though unique, are means to assist each member of our global family with the truth of their innate divinity. Our hearts are our divine connection to Spirit. Every soul knows that its origin is divine, whether they speak the language of divinity or not. Now I have a belief in an inclusive, unconditionally loving God, and my journey with Spirit has blessed me with freedom to be eclectic. Eclectic is defined as "consisting of components of diverse sources or styles." The beauty of being eclectic in my journey of faith has blessed me with the desire to stretch my once tight, exclusive theological headband until it completely fell off. I choose to honor and respect all faith traditions in their religare – reconnection – practices.

While on the subject of faith, here is a wonderful quote from *The New Possibility Thinker's Bible*: "Faith is a choice, not an argument. It is a decision, not a debate. It is a commitment, not a controversy. Faith fulfills some need in your heart."

The gift of free will provides each soul with the choice to incorporate into their journey of faith that which resonates as truth. Rev. Mary Manin Morrissey spoke about knowing what is true for each individual when she said, "We are all equipped with truth meters and our souls tell us when we are reading the truth. There is a light in us that responds to the light of truth and you can trust that light within you."

Meditation exercise

How do I know when my inner truth meter is sending a signal to me? Here is an exercise if you wish to create a more formal approach to discerning truth for yourself in order to develop trust in your own intuitive heritage.

Be quiet and be still. Take in a few long slow inhalations and exhalations. Focus your attention on the very centre of your head. To assist you to locate the centre of your head, envision two lines. One line will run from the front of your head, from the bridge of your nose through to the back of your head. A second line from one side of your head to the other, behind your eyes. Consider the intersection point to be an internal position of neutrality. Now breathe deeply and consciously into this spot. Once you feel comfortable in this neutral zone, ask for your wise aspect to provide you with a symbol you can use in the practice of providing yourself with more clarity. Be still, be quiet, and allow yourself time to receive a response.

In the request for a symbol, you are asking for a tool to use when you are unsure. Once you have received a symbol – which can be a shape, a sound, a color, a scent, a feeling, a sensation, or a movement of the body – you can test the symbol. Ask something you know to be a truth and the symbol can react and respond in confirmation of the truth. Then ask something you know is not true, and the symbol can not respond. Recognize, of course, that this symbol provides you with support in your discernment of truth and falsity, and it is a specific tool for personal use.

When I read, see, hear, or experience a truth, I receive a sensation in my body. The sensation at times is so strong that it is accompanied by miniature bumps on the surface of my skin, with the fine hair on my arms, legs, and neck standing straight up. God created the human body, and a miraculous messenger it is indeed! I am so grateful for this symbol, and I affectionately call it the "Holy Spirit Rush."

Conditioned belief in perfection

There is an obsession within our society with perfection and the media idealize the perfect body image. Some of us live in the world very self-consciously. Perfection-addicts, you're not alone!

There are those who are born with some challenges in life, and they are beacons of hope for the rest of us. I know a woman who was born with a stiff left hand and wrist. You can only imagine the cruel comments this soul endured during her life, especially the bullying during her early childhood when she did not look like all the other, supposedly normal, children. The truth is that there are no two of us the same!

This particular women did not allow her labeled disability to prohibit her from excelling in and living a rich, full, long life. She was a gifted artist and crocheted thousands of dollies, table-coverings, clothes, and gift items during her ninety-two years of life. She gave birth to and raised five children. She made all her own bread, buns, cakes, and cooked for herself up until she was ninety years of age. She had a memory that was absolutely impeccable. She would visit a home, take in the entire color scheme and interior decorations, and later, when an opportunity presented itself, she would gift the people who occupied the home with handmade crocheted items that perfectly matched their decor. This woman had plenty of time to take in her surroundings because others would not give her the time of day. She was, in many cases, treated like an outcast and not included in games or conversations, purely due to the unskilled, uncomfortable, reactionary behavior of those in her present company.

I learned a valuable lesson about this and my own igno-rance. During one season of my life I had a career that took me into people's homes to teach and do demonstrations and business transactions. At the conclusion of each evening I would invariably invite people to host another evening at their home at a mutually convenient time. After one such evening I received a phone call at my home from a woman I had met the night before. She asked me why I had not asked her to host a presentation. She had noted that I had asked everyone except her. That was absolutely right. I had assumed that because she was in a wheelchair she would not be able, nor would she want to, host a function in her home. What a silly mistake I made, because of an assumption. I learned an invaluable lesson that day. Just because someone looks different does not mean they are not brilliant and capable. Just because a person has a physical challenge to live with doesn't mean they do not enjoy entertaining and friendship. This woman was so gracious and kind that it made it easy for me to apologize for my discrimination. She invited me to facilitate a fundraising event that she hosted at her local activity centre. She taught me a lot about honoring yourself by speaking up, about forgiveness and mercy, about respect and friendship and charity. I was grateful to learn an invaluable lesson through an earth angel in a wheelchair.

Is bullying simply a symptom of our learned obsession with perfection? Does this obsession fuel our thoughts of discrimination, prejudice, and intolerance?

I have experienced bullying, discrimination, and preju- dice in my life and it is certainly a process to feel, deal and heal. In my hike of life adventure, I can now say to all those bullies in my life experiences: "Thank you for the physical, emotional, mental, and spiritual challenges. I would never have drawn from the wellspring of courage within and utilised it. I would not have developed such a large compas- sionate heart. Plus, I would never have learned that I am capable of creating a life-giving loving relationship with myself regardless of external circumstances.

Then the next phase in my hike of life adventure was an objective conscious review in order to empower myself to break the cycle of perpetuating the bullying against myself.

In addition, I became aware of and identified the impact of my descrimination and prejudice in my interpersonal relationships.

The cave of separation

Judgments, criticisms, and limiting thoughts about self and

others keep us in our heads and separate us from each other. The good news is that when we make the decision to take responsibility for our thoughts, we can transform them. If we diligently tell ourselves the microscopic truth about our thoughts, in time we can free ourselves from this form of, and the re-enactment of, violence in our lives.

Each time you observe destructive inner dialogue, you can stop and replace the negative or destructive thought by affirming: "I am, he is, she is, a divine creation." Plus, we can choose a positive constructive thought each time we're tempted to judge, criticize, or ridicule a member of our soul family. *Unity* magazine offered this idea in one of their publications: "I am, you are, we are, all students of life, always learning and gathering wisdom from situations as they occur!" Also, "God's love for us ensures we always have a new opportunity to succeed!"

Just for fun, I invite you to place this book in one hand or put it down for just a minute. Now with one arm extended from your shoulder straight out in front of you, point using just your index finger. You'll notice that your thumb automatically touches and even holds the other fingers against your palm. Still pointing your index finger, flip your hand over. This is a simple visual of what we do when we think a judgmental, critical, blaming thought about someone else. You'll notice that there are three fingers pointing back at you. So whatever it is you're thinking about someone else, whatever message you want to direct or say to someone else, it's three times more powerful for you. It's three times more powerful because you think it, say it, and hear it. The real-life lesson to learn is that the other soul is offering a gift by being a mirror, so that you become conscious of your thoughts, actions, and behaviors. I bet this perception is a little less easy for you to entertain, isn't it?

Personal example

Let me explain this with a personal example of the full cycle of the energy of separation. Within a week, I experienced separation in a dramatic way so that I would understand the energy of separation. The first opportunity came, delivered by a soul as a result of her judgment of me from two years previously. Then came a separation experience, as a result of me judging someone else from an accumulation that spanned a couple decades. Then came the judgment I had held of myself for nearly four decades.

In the first case, when I was judged by someone else, in my mind I separated myself from her when I thought how angry I was, how betrayed I felt, that she would bring this up when it had happened two years earlier. I relived all the drama and pain of not being accepted, of being criticized, even though we were both supposed members of a support group. My hurt feelings were because support to me then meant that I bring the real me, warts and all, and I would be accepted. Plus, with respect to confidentiality, I did believe I was not the subject for discussion by others in the group when I was not around.

When I nursed, cursed, and rehearsed this separation experience, I felt betrayed, suspicious, resentful, and distrusting. The more I clung to these thoughts, the stronger my emotions and the deeper the chasm I was creating between me and this soul. The impact of my thoughts created yucky energy between us that was actually palpable.

The truth for me to see and learn through this experience of separation was: "When had I done this to others? When had I given my unsolicited opinion? When had I been so focused on the behavior of others that it kept me too busy to work through my own issues? Who am I to point out the issue someone else needs to work on, in my opinion, and rob them of coming to the decision to make changes in their lives when it suited them? When had I not honored confidentiality? When had I gossiped?"

Something else I learned was that I had been attempting to meet all my support needs in one place. I learned through this experience that it was time for me to define for myself what support meant to me and what I envisioned it to be. I became willing to determine in which areas of my life I wanted and needed support. I could ask the appropriate people to co-create support with me, and this allowed me to enlarge my support circle. I created agreements with specific people where our connection would be mutually beneficial and the energy of support was life-giving, not toxic.

Then I experienced separation as a result of my judgment of someone else. I had kept score and held my tongue for years – in truth, for decades. I had repeatedly betrayed myself and gone away hurt and angry. Meanwhile, this soul would say whatever was on her mind without thinking about the impact her words had upon others. I was presented with an opportunity to finally speak my truth in a life-giving way and bring to the table what I had held onto for such a long time. Do note that if you ever decide to do this, be forewarned. Just because you're ready to talk, doesn't mean that others are ready to listen. Just because you come with a heart of reconciliation doesn't mean that others will not be defensive and argumentative. Just because you are willing to set clear boundaries of what is open for discussion and what is not doesn't mean it will be well received. Understanding and wisdom come through experience, and if you are committed to growing, you will manage to pass through the awkward phases when practicing. The reward is the creation of a real, deep, and meaning-filled manner of relating.

The thought that produced my emotions in this instance was an invitation to acknowledge and deal with my jealousy, keeping of scores, competitiveness, tit-for-tat approach, bitterness, and revenge. What an opportunity to own the consequences of my thoughts and feelings, and to observe my actions and experiences. Through this process I identified how I could create new and different results. I had to first be willing to make the necessary changes and manage my own thoughts differently. It is certainly ludicrous, in my experience, to expect someone else to change so that I will think rightly.

Then I experienced separation as a result of my judgment of myself. One Sunday morning, I saw one of the individuals who participated in my teenage sexual abuse experience, in a local restaurant with his daughter. Did that send me into a momentary mental tailspin? You can say that again. I shot silent mental darts at him. I wanted to go over to the table and say to the girl that I hoped she never experiences at the hands of boys in her life what I experienced at her father's hands. I wanted to tell him how much he had ruined my life and my ability to be intimate in relationships. I wanted to tell him how angry I was for the consequence of not telling anyone and the resulting destructive self-abuse through all my addictions. He must have felt the energy of my toxic, angry thoughts because he changed seating places with his daughter. When it came time for me to pay my bill, I had to walk right past them. I felt a mixture of anger, terror, and panic, so I stayed put at the table to silently pray for support to open my heart to them both. The gift for me was that when I went over and asked if he was who I thought he was, he responded, "Yes," and introduced me to his daughter. I looked at her and said, "Oh, _____, you are so beautiful." We talked briefly and at the end of our conversation I shook hands with him.

The healing that came from this exchange for me was that when I keep my heart open and the love energy flows out to others, I feel it too. *Heartmath* had given me a new perception with regard to forgiveness, which I had just put into practice: "Love is for giving." What continued to repeat in my mind was the phrase "You are so beautiful," and I kept seeing her young, sweet, innocent face. Over and over I saw it, until I finally accepted this as truth for myself. When I was her age, I too was "so beautiful," and I too was innocent and sweet. It was then that I turned a corner in the hike of my life adventure with regards to my teenage sexual abuse experiences. Affirming my beauty, sweetness, and innocence, I could learn to believe it when I looked at myself in the mirror. With this new awareness, consistent practice, and divine assistance, I could surrender the limiting belief that "I was used goods, forever tarnished." They were labels that I'd burdened myself with for so long.

The main real-life lesson I learned was that when I am in my head giving energy to judgment and criticism, I believe in separation. When I am in my heart, then I believe and give energy to the truth of the innate divinity in others. I was learning to activate and consciously utilize both my heart and brain systems of intelligence coherently.

Another real-life lesson I learned was that, with each judgmental, critical thought, I create a veil, like a lens in an imaginary pair of glasses. I perceive and look at whomever through the lens of _____ [fill in the blank with the word that best describes your judgment – anger, resentment, jealousy, envy, etc.]. Each time I make a judgmental, critical thought, I add another lens. In the three aforementioned examples I was looking through multiple lenses – the lenses of betrayal, distrust, suspiciousness, resentment, jealousy, envy, keeping score, competitiveness, bitterness, self-condemnation, self-criticism, anger, and self-hate.

Do you see and understand how your view of people becomes warped when you walk about attempting to see through such an accumulation of contaminated lenses? Look at how I perceived and saw others and myself as a consequence of my thoughts. I encourage you to tell yourself the microscopic truth about the lenses you create with your thoughts and your perceptions as a result. The full cycle of the energy of separation is an experience of choice.

The cave of conflict

In the past, during my formal schooling years, I was not taught conflict resolution. In my experience of life, I learned that if you had a disagreement, a falling out, or an all-out fight, the relationship was over and that you or the other person(s) involved would leave. Harsh words spoken are not easily forgotten are they? How many times have you given someone a piece of your mind, when you'd have been better off keeping it to yourself? My experience of conflict created in me a pattern of "wanting to avoid it at all cost."

I had the privilege to tour a school a few years back that prominently displayed an incredible poster by Robert E. Vallett. On it he offered a step-by-step approach to "Peaceful

Conflict Resolution." Using the acronym "RESOLUTION," Vallett shares his recipe: "Respect the right to disagree. Express your real concerns. Share common goals and interests. Open yourself to different points of view. Listen carefully to all proposals. Understand the major issues involved. Think about probable consequences. Imagine several possible alternative solutions. Offer some reasonable compromises. Negotiate a mutually fair cooperation. We are all one family under the same sky." I would advocate that this poster be hung in every school, office, and home so the visual would remind individuals to practice, practice, practice this recipe. Can you imagine the difference this would make in the lives of all who were willing to work with it?

While exploring the cave of conflict, I told myself the truth of how covert avoidance energy can be in a relationship when not addressed. I realized how paranoid I had become when relating to others. It was staggering when I became conscious of the regularity of my own suspicious thoughts. I was investing a lot of energy into obsessing about the motive and intent of others. Obviously, my past had a lot to do with this, and the truth for me was that I had huge betrayal and abandonment issues to work through. Consequently, I was gauging my adult relationships using a warped, wounded child meter. I measured present experiences up against past circumstances. It was very enlightening to realize how suspicion easily escalated into a paranoid fantasy based on my hyper-vigilance and mistaken perceptions. I heard a wonderful analogy of mistake, which I invite you to consider and integrate into your life if you choose.

When you observe yourself in a relationship challenge, look through the lens of your life and pause on the frame of your mistaken perception. Tell yourself the truth, and take responsibility for the perception, because it is the result of the thoughts coming from the projector of your mind. This is the process of owning and taking responsibility for your mistake on this clip from your life experience. Silent observation and reflection time is a wonderful gift to give yourself. Writing about the event will assist you in developing a life-giving relationship with yourself.

The pause can be your choice to ask for clarification and your willingness to check something out with the individual(s) involved. When I think a suspicious thought, I create and contribute to separation energy between myself and the other(s) involved. When I do this, I rob myself and others of the opportunity of making an intimate connection. When this occurs, I splinter the sacred trust in this relationship. When I'm in my head I separate myself from others by my very thoughts. When I'm in my heart, and I keep it open, I feel connected with others. To remedy a situation of this sort takes practice. It also takes courage to free yourself from the habitual ways of being in relationships.

Personal example

On one occasion I asked a friend, "Are you willing to be courageous with me? When I said _____, I saw a look on your face, then I heard _____. What did you mean? I'm curious and would like to understand, so I don't create distance between us by allowing my misperception to feed an exaggerated disaster story in my head. The relationship I have with you is important to me."

This is a method of approaching a relationship with the

heart of reconciliation. The aforementioned exercise is a response-able technique of mental and emotional self-management. It nurtures a life-giving, loving, respect-filled relationship with self, because you honor your emotions and tell the truth about your actual thoughts. It is a method of honoring yourself without pointing the finger of blame and condemnation at another. When you point the finger of blame, it is a coping strategy to deny that the issue is yours, and an attempt to make it about the other person. Instead, practice taking ownership of the thoughts you choose to think. Thoughts precede emotions, actions, and results. Ask yourself, "What thoughts am I thinking that create the emotions I am feeling? What are the results I experience as a consequence of my thoughts, emotions, and actions?"

When you approach relationship challenges as opportunities to listen, learn, and grow in understanding for each other, your win/lose, right/wrong mentality loses its power. You learn that there is such a thing as compromise and that it is possible to move ahead with a consensus. You learn to accept that it is okay to let go of a stuck position on an issue and to agree to disagree. You may have different opinions and perceptions about an issue, topic, or value. It is not necessary to keep trying to convince each other that the way you see it is the correct way and that the way the other(s) see it is inappropriate. There can be a place of "no right and no wrong," where there are simply different perceptions and points of view.

I invite you to scan your life, to think of examples of relationship challenges when you projected your hurt feelings and emotions upon those about you; times when you attempted to make someone else responsible for them. Did you ever have an individual shake their finger at you and declare, "You make me so mad?" This confrontational, win/lose, blaming style of communication was learned, and perhaps you adopted and practiced it in your relationships. Thankfully, anything learned can be unlearned if and when you determine for yourself that it no longer serves you.

Example

I was going away for the weekend with some friends. Upon collecting our last travel companion, she shared how she'd burned herself a couple times in the last couple days. Louise L. Hay has written wonderful books on metaphysics, which I use as a resource to assist me in my desire to be response-able for my thoughts. *You Can Heal Your Life* and *Heal Your Body* are my favorites, as they contain tables that list problems, probable cause, and new thought-pattern affir-mation ideas. I have burned myself many times and was curious about the metaphysical interpretation, the "beyond the physical" perception of the thoughts that may con-tribute to the condition or symptom (burn) I experienced. This process, though regarded as simplistic by some people, has been extremely beneficial for me. I highly recommend you check out these books for yourself and allow your inner truth meter to decide.

In my personal investigation I read: "Burns – anger, burning up, incensed." Then the suggested affirmation read: "I create only peace and harmony within myself and in my environment. I deserve to feel good."

During the weekend this woman shared many stories of her past experiences, which, honoring confidentiality, I am not at liberty to repeat. As the weekend neared completion, she began expressing her anger, which was directed toward others, including me. Thank goodness for my enhanced self-understanding of my own anger. I was able to listen to her vent her anger and I said silently to myself, "I am not responsible for my friend's anger." And then in response I said aloud, "I am not going to take this on."

What a long way I'd come in my ability to be with someone when they were angry, to simply be a sounding board or a mirror and allow their anger to be expressed. My past habit would be to try to fix it, try to make the other person feel better, or in some cases talk for them, to the person with whom they were angry. Or in the cases where someone dumped their anger on me, thinking I was responsible for their anger, I accepted it. Often I would run the tape over and over in my mind, with the words I could have used in my reaction. This limiting co dependent habit of believing that I can actually cause, or be held accountable for, the thoughts, feelings, actions, and beliefs of someone other than myself, had surfaced for healing. Don Miguel Ruiz, in his book *The Four Agreements*, states: "Nothing others do is because of me, it is a result of their own life experience and the events and circumstances from the past which are being triggered in the present."

Situations like this come forward for the purpose of healing. When you become aware of, and practice being response-able for, your thoughts, which create your emotions, you experience how relationship interactions can be mutually beneficial. At all times, you have the choice to feel, deal, and heal by revealing, or not revealing, the truth to yourself. You can deny and postpone the lesson until it comes up again. It will, until we ask, "What is this trying to teach me about me? I've been in this circumstance before.

What is the common denominator in these scenarios? Oh, what a surprise – it's me!"

You can ask your inner wise guidance, your divine nature, to assist you. The God of our understanding is an ever-present help. Your part is simply to ask and the door to new understanding will be opened. The healing energy of the divine will wash through your experience, and in the process you will be born anew in mind and heart.

The cave of the inner critic

I can only speak for myself here. I really do value constructive feedback – when I ask for it. We all have lessons to learn in our own time, when we're ready to learn them. When I give my unsolicited opinion about something to someone, I am not in truth honoring their intensely personal sacred soul journey. Having said that, there is another side to this coin that I experienced, which was a rather huge "ah-ha!" What I have learned about life up until now is that I am never alone in my experience. When I take the step of vulnerability and share with another, both of our lives are transformed.

I've been on the receiving end of feedback that was, in fact, judgment and criticism. Have you ever received feedback that was judgment and criticism, outside of your annual employee review through work? I have, many times, but one time in particular stands out because it was a verbal critical synopsis of my life. The situation derailed me emotionally for months. I nursed it, cursed it, and rehearsed it until I almost drove myself mad. Then, finally, I was willing to surrender my limited viewpoint and I prayed for divine assistance: "What is the lesson, what am I to learn from this? I do not ever want to experience this mental madness and emotion in this intensity again!"

Let me tell you, the answer was astounding – and what a miraculous new perception: "This individual did not say anything to you that you have not thought about yourself at one time or another." Was this hard for me to receive, accept, and believe? You can say that again. When I reviewed the verbal diatribe – this time with an open mind that was in alignment with my open, perceptive heart – it was absolutely true. My negative, judgmental, critical self-talk came forward to me through one intense relationship interaction, and grabbed my attention. The truth is, I had been doing affirmations for years and had totally disowned the fact that I had a huge inner critic. In the words of the late Dr. Sister Elsie, from Missoula, Montana, "You can't put whip cream on a cow pie!"

I had endured a harsh smack that some refer to as the "two-by-four chunk of wood, wake-up-call type of lesson," and I did not need another lesson of this magnitude to change the way I thought about myself. I would rather receive "the tickle of a feather wake-up-call type of lesson." Do I continue a practice of catching myself when I mentally berate myself? Absolutely! Not only do I stop myself through consistent silent observation, but I also practice aloud. When I catch myself thinking demeaning things about myself, I say, "Who just said that? It is just not true. I am a beloved, precious soul." I have done this also when in the company of someone else who verbally put themselves down. The verbal practice aloud is three times more powerful for us than the silent mental dialogue. Why? Because first you have to think it, then you have to say it, and then you have to hear it. So when I was in the company of a friend and they scolded themselves, I'd say, "Pardon me. Excuse me. Who just said that about my friend and dear soul _____ [fill in the blank with their name]. That is just not true. _____ is divine and wonderful in all aspects. _____ is a precious and beloved soul." You'll notice that you say the name of the individual three times. Advertisers say "the power of three" is the ratio for success. Why not test it out for yourself and see if the power of three works for you?

Each of us has a vulnerable aspect of self, which thrives in a life-giving, accepting environment. The vulnerable self wants unconditional support and freedom to express itself without being attacked verbally, emotionally, or energetically. When condemnation ideas are thought and not expressed verbally, their energy still has an impact on whoever, whatever, wherever they are directed.

To create life-giving, loving relationships, practice life-giving techniques that honor your self and others. This will naturally ripple out from you to others. Remember, it takes practice. The most important component is to be available to self, through silent conscious observation of your thoughts. Mental self-management will inevitably increase your self-awareness and self-understanding and your ability to develop a rapport relationship with yourself.

In my discussion of the topic and perception of cave experiences I gave specific examples from my own life. We all have cave experiences to deal with if we have ever kept a life experience a secret. The accumulation of these secrets means that we have a whole lot of energy in the dark cave of our unconscious and the idea of beaming your inner light into the cave means you are willing to bring the secret into the light of your conscious awareness. The beauty of the techniques I have described is that they can be adapted to your own real-life examples in order to appropriately meet your own needs. There is a light at the entrance to the cave, there is a light at the end of the tunnel, and this light is you. Your own innate, divine, inner light waits to be expressed and utilized, and with it the experience of your innate potentiality. Are you willing to deal with the caves in your life? Ask for support from others in your global family. You can do it!

That concludes our discussion of cave experiences. Return to the trail outside the cave and make your way to the ocean. When you reach the beach, continue to walk north away from the breakaway sandstone monolith. Soon you will see and approach a magnificent cove. The ocean is so serene that its surface is similar to that of a mirror.

Honor and Respect

Honor and respect
all expressions of Spirit,
No matter the form
in which you find it.
Billions of costumes
inhabit this planet,
So honor and respect
all expressions with love.

Mirror Experiences

Imagination exercise

I invite you to stare at the pillow-soft white clouds suspended in the blue sky, containing a wide variety of shapes, including even a few faces looking up into the heavens. Allow your eyes to go slightly out of focus, and continue to look at the clouds in the sky, reflected upon the surface of the calm, still ocean. You'll notice there is little to no impulse to blink your eyes. Your breathing slows down and it aligns with the rhythm of your heartbeat. You may feel as though your heart is beating inside and outside of your physical body simultaneously. You are completely attuned to the energy of the present moment in this open-eye meditation experience. In this receptive, open state I offer you some new perceptions.

Are you willing to consider for a moment that nature has a message for you? Could this scene be an invitation from nature to entertain the mirror analogy with regard to your personal and professional relationship interactions? It's easy to embrace this new perception of "relationship as mirror" when the relationship is pleasant. I bet your hesitancy to adopt and practice this new perception comes from an aspect of self that argues, "You mean that this principle is for all relationships, even the ones that are a pain?" Yes, the new perception is intended for your consideration with regard to all interpersonal relationships.

When you are smack dab in the middle of a real-life relationship challenge, you may be less willing to consider the implications of it as a mirror. Some relationship interactions present you with challenges that pack a power-filled punch, which triggers an inner reaction. It is the inner reaction that is your signal to pay attention. There is a lesson in this relationship mirror coming to you as teacher, if you're willing to see it by telling yourself the truth. Yes, you have a choice. You can choose to continue to deny that which someone else is mirroring to you is actually an aspect of how you show up in the world or an aspect of self you may have disowned. The opportunity is for you to choose to be present with yourself, increase your conscious awareness, by asking: "What is this relationship or nature mirror wanting to teach me about me?" When you make time to perceive how the relationship or nature mirror has relevance and provides clarity in your own life, you receive wonder.

You are being encouraged by the stimulation to make necessary changes by adopting new perceptions. These new perceptions are the very beginning of telling yourself the truth about something that you may have not been willing to face up to until now. Denial is a coping strategy for remaining unconscious and unwilling to see what there is for you to see. Denial may also be a way of protecting yourself when you are not ready to deal with what is being mirrored to you. Denial keeps you safe in a self-imposed comfort zone. In order to move beyond a self-imposed comfort zone, you may need to change your thoughts about yourself and/or others. Denial also keeps you in victim consciousness, and allows you to defer being response-able for your thoughts, attitudes, behaviors, or beliefs.

In order to practice this technique, it is important to

create a new habit of silent personal self-observation time, to be curious about the judgments and criticisms you make of others. In order for you to identify and acknowledge something in someone else, you must be familiar with it first-hand. Otherwise, how else could you label, identify, and recognize it?

Are you having trouble with this notion? Feeling uncomfortable? Hang in there, this is good – it means change is coming. You are blessed with limitless opportunities each day, through your interactions with billions of soul brothers and sisters, animals, and nature. The truth, if you are willing to accept it, is that we are all teachers of, and learners from, each other, regardless of age. So when you consciously acknowledge yourself thinking or speaking a judgment or criticism, stop and silently ask yourself the following.

"What is this teaching me about me?"
"What is this person mirroring back for me to
   see about me?"
"What is it about this person that is so repulsive
   or annoying?"
"What am I resisting, what part of my energetic
   expression have I disowned?"

You'll learn volumes – it takes courage and willingness to tell yourself the microscopic truth.

Each time a person acts as a mirror to you, and you accept the lesson being so generously offered to you, there can be merriment. You are in the process of bringing awareness to a splintered part of your energetic expression from unconscious to conscious, and there is joy in that, is there not? There is always gold in a lesson if you're willing to mine it. A play on words, the phrase "mine it" can be a humorous anecdote to remind us to take responsibility for self. It takes practice to realize personal self-management. We have heaps of soul brothers and sisters with whom to practice.

Do you recall the exercise when I invited you to raise one arm, lock your elbow, and point using only your index finger? There is great significance in the meaning of this hand gesture as it relates to the mirror analogy. Whenever you point a finger at someone else fueled by a judgment or criticism, there are three fingers pointing back at you. When you speak the judgment or criticism aloud, then the lesson is three times more powerful for you. Why? First you have to think it, then you say it, and then you hear it. So the message is a powerful one, bouncing off the relationships mirror and coming back at you threefold, when initially you thought you were making a point. Get it? Whatever it is, that is what is coming up, which has more to do with you than it does with the other person.

You have the choice, to deal with it as a real-life lesson and learn, grow, and change as a result of the powerful reflection in the mirror, or you can defer learning the lesson until later. "The lesson will be repeated until you learn the lesson." What I have learned through experience is that it may come from a new mirror (new relationship), but it will be the same lesson.

Personal story of working with the idea

I had the privilege of working with this mirror concept as a result of reading Shakti Gawain's book, *Path of*

Transformation. Then I participated in a one-week intensive course that Shakti facilitated in order to practice the technique. Here's what I learned.

Whenever I feel comfortable in the company of another individual, it is because the person is expressing energy that I am comfortable expressing. When I am not comfortable in the company of another, then the opportunity is for me to label, by silent observation, what it is this person is mirroring to me. The intensity of the mirror is equal to the degree to which I had disowned this energetic expression within myself.

During the intensive course, I was asked to look at my key relationships and ask myself, "Is there a characteristic about this individual that really perturbs me? Is there something about them that I really dislike? Is there something about them that makes me really uncomfortable?" The purpose of the questions is to identify what it is? When I initially did this truth-telling evaluation exercise with my key life-relationship, it proved to be most beneficial. The characteristics and personality traits that became it for me, and that I was going to consciously work with were impersonal, anger, victim, and emotional energetic expressions of self. I'll explain how I worked with each issue in detail.

Example – impersonal energy mirror

I realized through self-study that I had a limiting belief about impersonal energy. I am a very sensitive being (the truth is that we all are) and when I was younger I concluded that impersonal energy hurt people. It was cold, it was harsh, it was standoffish, and if people were like this around me it probably meant that they did not like me. I adopted this limiting belief and unique perception about impersonal energy in my youth. This new exercise made it clear to me that this belief from my youth about impersonal energy no longer served me as an adult.

The truth is, I need impersonal energetic expression in order to be effective in business and personal relationships. I had totally disowned expressing this energy, and through this relationship mirror as teacher, the invitation was for me to bring it (impersonal energy) into a workable balance in my personality expression. A workable balance in my life for me meant utilizing both my personal and impersonal energy. Up until this conscious realization, the majority of time I was totally invested in operating in the world using primarily my personal energy. What I learned was to finally start owning my impersonal energy, and practicing express-ing it, especially in business situations. I began to free myself from a destructive habit of taking things so personally. My habit of perceiving the actions of others and taking them to heart, as I did as an impressionable child, crippled me in adult interactions. It was not until I got to the root core issue (that impersonal energy hurt people), that I was able to con-sciously choose to surrender this limiting belief. Equipped with fresh understanding and conscious access to my own impersonal expression, I was empowered to create more life-giving relationships.

Exercise

Imagine yourself with people in your life who are playful, affectionate, make direct eye contact, listen to you, and talk with you. Through their interactions and conversations with you, it is as though they come into your world, and you feel the connection both energetically and emotionally. This is a rough description of a personal energy connection in relationship.

On the other end of the spectrum, imagine yourself with people in your life who are busy, preoccupied with the immediate task at hand, and driven to complete, or those with a focus on doing more than being. Perhaps these people set very good clear boundaries energetically and do not get enmeshed with others through touching or direct eye contact. These individuals are more prone to broach small talk to keep conversations on the surface of safe subjects that are not of a personal or emotional nature. This is a brief outline of some of the characteristics of an intellectual, impersonal connection.

From your experience of these exercises, and your real-life relationship interactions, you will come to understand the difference between impersonal and personal energy expression. You will determine for yourself, through self-observation, whether the two are out of balance. Occasionally, I still get twinges when I am in the presence of someone who is extremely impersonal, and this indicates to me that there is room for more healing through practice. The twinges are encouraging compared to the depression and emotional derailment I experienced in the past. In working with many of the ideas contained within this hike of life adventure, this may be your experience as well. You know that the ideas are working and you are growing and transforming by the sense of yourself as a result of your practice of a particular technique. Your results are not physical, tangible evidence of all your hard work, yet you may be more aware and more calm, more balanced and less reactionary, than you were in the past. You experience a measurable difference in your own knowledge, wisdom, and your understanding of yourself through your experiences.

Example – anger energy mirror

Another energetic expression that I was extremely uncomfortable with was anger. As a youth I determined that anger was loud, it hurt people, it was ugly, and it equaled violence. In my life I had disowned my anger by being nice, nice, nice all the time. I invested my energy in being the doer, the pleaser, the skilled manipulator, and the controller in order to keep the peace. I used a series of pretty drastic measures to fulfill a desperate need for comfort and safety. Through self-study I discovered that I went to great lengths to avoid anger. In my youth I had learned that angry children were sent away, and were abandoned. I adopted the belief that my anger was unacceptable and that if someone else became very frustrated and angry they would abandon me by leaving, whether temporarily by slamming a door, or altogether. This left me feeling unworthy.

Anger energy, when viewed as destructive, has been likened to that of a volcano. When a volcano erupts it spews hot cinder and ash that burns and consumes everything in its path. Molten red-hot lava flows and burns everything, then dries black leaving its permanent imprint. Anger, like lava, collects and flows through lava tubes beneath the surface, building up pressure, creating steam, seeking to release itself. When it does surface it explodes, creating smoke as it hits the atmosphere. A volcano can have devastating results, which can be heard and seen from a distance. People run to avoid it. It is life-threatening.

Anger, when viewed as natural, normal, healthy emotional energy, can be acknowledged and expressed constructively with response-ability. Anger can also be a motivational force that acts as a catalyst to create the momentum for an individual to make positive personal changes in their lives. When life circumstances or particular situations annoy us, anger can be what propels us to be creative and make necessary lifestyle changes. Mother Earth in action in the form of a volcano is a creative force. She is in a constant state of flux, recreating herself every moment. And so it is with us.

Personal experience

Here's a real-life lesson I learned with regard to anger. It came forward to me in a very intense way. I was gifted with the opportunity to work with a man who some referred to as a tyrant. The idea of tyrant speaks to me, because I feel that a good deal of energy in my life has been dedicated to the practice of honoring and taming my tyrant within, rather than completely denying it. During the time I made a contribution to the organization, his anger disturbed me continuously. I had plenty of time to work through my anger issues. It was interesting to note how he used anger in an attempt to control everyone and everything. The entire team would go to great lengths to avoid the wrath of his anger. A part of me would contract when I heard, through the walls, each time his anger erupted in the workplace. This was a gift to me in the sense that I finally began to acknowledge the fact that I was human and I too felt anger.

My habitual pattern up until then had been not to express my anger externally. It had to go somewhere, and in my case I fed this feeling. I stuffed it down, I chewed and chewed and chewed. I swallowed it. I turned it inward against myself and this had some drastic consequences. Not only was my health in jeopardy because I gained fifty pounds, but I also discovered I was growing cysts, fibroid tumors, because of the anger toxin I was storing within. I did have surgery to remove the growths and they were not malignant. I literally had physical representations of my anger cut out of me.

I was presented with the opportunity to learn to deal effectively with my anger. I read books on the subject and practiced anger releasing techniques. I listened to audio recordings and practiced anger releasing meditations. I took anger management courses. I practiced speaking the truth of my anger, with regular visits to a counselor, taking responsibility for it by journalizing and allowing it to vent, to run its course. And amazingly, when I started to take responsibility for my own anger, I no longer felt responsible for anyone else's anger.

I knew I had made progress when on one occasion I had someone standing and raging and pointing a finger of blame at me. I let the person finish. Then, fully composed, centered, and in the present with myself, I replied, in a calm, clear voice while making direct eye contact, "_____ [fill in the blank with the person's name], that is just not true." The individual doing the raging could hardly believe their ears, because from the look on their face, it appeared that I had hit them with a laser beam from a stun gun. Their anger is theirs, their thoughts and perceptions are theirs, and I am not a garbage pail for others to use as a dumpster.

Compassion allowed me to perceive, under all that anger, a tormented person in a lot of pain. I am not responsible for their pain or for fixing it. Talk about the beginning of freedom from a destructive habitual way of always trying to smooth out a volatile environment or just walking away. There had been many anger mirrors along the way. I had avoided them. This extremely intense anger mirror made it impossible for me to avoid dealing with my anger any longer. In order to survive in the workplace I invested time to research and learn how to acknowledge and creatively express my own anger. The intensity of a relationship mirror is equal to the degree to which I have disowned the particular energetic expression within myself.

Example – victim mirror

I have met so many people kind enough to be my victim mirror. "Life happens to me, poor me, I'm so hard done by, and people always take advantage of me." Behind my victim mentality was resentment. Re-sent anger. I could nurse, curse, and rehearse my past rather than feel, deal, and heal it by revealing the truth about the situation to myself. I could tell myself the truth about what was really going on for me. I could tell myself the truth about what I needed and wanted and expected to be happening but which wasn't. I realized that if I desired things to be different then I must change, rather than expect society or someone else to change. I had to admit to myself that playing the part of victim kept me stuck, and I could whine, complain, explain, and justify my position all I wanted, to distract myself from changing. I could be a victim and try to get others to agree with me and give me the desired sympathy. I could even get others to help me with the problem and even take it on and deal with it for me so that I wouldn't have to. By perpetuating my victim role I could extend the pity party, so I could stay in my self-imposed victim comfort zone.

What did I learn? That life does not happen to me, and I had spent enough time believing that it did. Thoughts contribute volumes to my experience because my thoughts are energy. When I create new thoughts I create new and different results. If, in a present moment, I am not experiencing what I'd like in my health, wealth, relationships, or career, then I have to stop being the victim. To move out of victim, I must first admit that I think I am one. From this place of acceptance, I own how my victim thoughts have contributed to the creation of the condition being experienced. Here is a saying I have read in a couple of different ways through reading *Science of Mind* and *Unity* writings, which I have paraphrased and put in the first person singular, and you may wish to use it as an affirmation: "Change my thinking – change my life."

Example – emotional mirror

Have you had any emotional souls in your life? I have had many souls speak their feelings and thoughts out loud and usually rather dramatically. Are you a drama addict or do you have any drama addicts in your life? Frequently, my initial impulse was that I was turned off by (in my limited opinion) their overreaction. I had always been turned off by their dramatization. I had always been turned off by their vulnerability. Wow, what a wake-up call to realize that what had turned me off, I had actually turned off within me. The emotional mirror was intense because I had disowned my emotional feeling nature. As a child, being vulnerable in the company of others had disastrous consequences, as did being emotional and speaking my feelings out loud. So I had learned to shut down, to stay safe in abusive and volatile environments.

I learned to be self-reliant and strong to give others the impression I could look after myself. I prided myself on being very independent. What I did was abandon myself and betray my own feelings and emotional nature. There is not too much that is more painful than betrayal or abandonment of self. The glitch was that I had learned to do this and it affected the relationship with myself, and all my relationships.

Learning to be vulnerable with myself and allow myself to feel and acknowledge my emotions was an incredible journey. First came the practice of acknowledging my feelings. Second, I began to give myself permission to allow the energy of my emotions to run its course through constructive expression as guided by my intuition. Third, through silent observation of myself in my relationship interactions I began to take responsibility for how I felt in the moment and acknowledged my emotions. During the course of this type of self-study I came to understand how the thoughts I choose to think create my feelings, which in turn affect my action or inaction, and this creates the results I experience.

Example – self-centered mirror

Another mirror that was repeatedly shown to me by people was the self-centered mirror. The self-centered mirror showed me how at times I acted as though the world revolved around me. As if my needs and desires were more important than others and I should not have to wait my turn in line-ups – I wanted what I wanted, when I wanted it, and not when it was mutually convenient. I saw clearly that "me, me, me" was not a very honorable chant. When I was willing to admit the frequency of the self-centered mirror, I asked, "What is my limiting root core belief that fuels my self-centered behavior?"

My answer was "fear of not enough," "I'll not get mine." Then there were also my beliefs that there is not enough time, not enough attention, not enough money, and not enough love. These were the layers in my self-study that led to my understanding of my belief in a win/lose mentality. I would barter and bargain for goods and services to get the best price, while not honoring the one providing the service or the goods. I had become obsessed with getting. The impact of this mirror came home to me when I was not valued in a contract negotiation and I was not treated with respect, and the contract was not completely honored per our agreement.

There were huge mirrors with regard to focusing on price (when I believed in lack of money) and I did not acknowledge value, skill, and ability. This was certainly a bitter pill to swallow. The truth was that when I focused only on satisfying my needs (a win/lose strategy and "take, take, take" mentality), I was oblivious and gave no conscious thought to the needs or concerns of anyone else. I was focused on the result and cared much less about the consequences of my actions, as long as I came out winning.

This became particularly clear when I was involved in commissioned sales and entrepreneurial ventures. I had been so focused on the win, the sale, the strategic alliance, that I would push to get my needs met, oversell, and actually annoy people with whom I desired to do business or network.

Self-centeredness manifests in a limiting belief in superiority

One mirror was a wealthy soul who constantly beat people down in price to get what was required. The mirror was the lack of appreciation, gratitude, and value placed upon the contributions of others. The limiting belief was that material wealth, social status, or intellectual knowledge made them superior, more deserving, and of more value. I certainly did not want to believe, nor was I proud to admit, that I did this as well. What a tragic way to live. I was invested in a constant struggle of win/lose rather than a cooperative, creative win/win in relationships with people and with the environment. Have you ever behaved as though you believed you were superior? Have you ever been on a power trip where you bossed others around and told them what to do without treating them with dignity and respect? Is respect a two-way street in your relationship interactions?

Self-centeredness in relationship dynamics

A group of friends attended a community event together. Some couples and some singles. At one point a single individual sat down to socialize with a woman who had arrived at the event, part of a couple. These two individuals had a lovely visit with each other. The woman's partner was not impressed at all, and later the woman shared with me how this had disturbed her partner. His expectations were, "You come together, you sit together, and you leave together." Well, this triggered within me a reaction. I had partnered with an individual, some twenty-five years earlier, who was self-centered, possessive, jealous, insecure, and controlling. Although he was no longer in my life, this simple sharing of information triggered my thoughts, and the consequence was a replay of many similar unpleasant situations from my past. I was on a mental tailspin, nursing, cursing, and rehearsing the past. I also noted that I was so uncomfortable in my body – the pain was almost unbearable for a number of days. I was very curious about the pain and in a quiet meditative state I inquired, "What's all this pain about?"

The answer came in snapshots from my life of all the times I had been self-centered, possessive, jealous, insecure, and controlling in my relationships, from childhood all the way to the present. A limiting belief that no longer served me was coming up for me to release. A belief in lack of love, not enough attention, having to have my social needs met, win/lose without consideration of anyone else. This realization stung a bit as I silently reviewed the wake of my broken friendships and relationships. My unconscious limiting beliefs and thoughts had contributed to the breakdown of so many of my relationships, when I had not taken responsibility for the part I had played in the disintegration of the relationship. As an unconscious victim, my coping mechanism was to retreat and become isolated from social situations. This invariably meant despondency, depression, and a binge of some description. This was the consequence of denying that it was my thoughts, and of my unrealistic expectations of others meeting my needs for love and security.

This was indeed a habit pattern I wanted to shift, and gradually over time it is transforming as I change my thoughts. I still experience twinges, particularly in my interactions with family. For instance, if a sibling receives something and I do not. This tells me I'm a work-in-progress and the road to successful life-giving interpersonal relationships is always under construction.

Perception of self-centeredness on the road

Is the road rage phenomenon we hear so much about in the news the epitome of self-centeredness? Driving is a privilege and we very obviously share the road with millions of others. No, my appointment is not more important than anyone else's. Yes, it is better I drive at a safe speed – I may be late, but I'll be alive. Would I prefer to arrive composed and relaxed or stressed out and harried?

Although I have practiced much to tame my self-centeredness when driving, I still observe circumstances of when I leak my energy in destructive reactions to less than courteous actions of other drivers. Oh well, the road to success is always under construction. At least now I am more conscious of my own behaviors and thoughts and can choose alternative life, giving thoughts.

Taming road rage suggestions

If you commute every day, I offer you several suggestions if you wish to make some changes during your traveling time. Make your vehicle into a mobile peace parlor by playing suitable music. At other times, make your vehicle into your mobile university by listening to educational or positive, inspiring, informative cassettes. Enjoy a season of learning when driving, rather than listening to the news and focusing on the traffic. You may like to chant or sing in the privacy of your own vehicle during your commute. Be in joy without caring what other drivers think. Perhaps you may wish to make it your practice to drive and be silent. This may be the only time of solitude you have in the day. What about filling your commute time with a series of your daily appreciations and gratitudes for the beauty of nature, for the people in your life, and the fond memories you have created?

It is not a requirement for any of us to participate in the self-centered road rage of anyone else. You are not responsible for their impatience and anger, and need not get hooked by it. Rather than react with the one-finger salute, be creative and proactive. Instead, smile and consciously beam a stream of light and/or peace energy from your heart in the direction of the other driver. Do you know what happens when you throw a boomerang? It comes back to you. However, using this analogy it does not necessarily come back to you from the same person in your present circumstance. So remember that your thoughts are energy and whatever you put out comes back to you, in some form. If there is a traffic accident during your commute, why not pause and pray for those involved rather than focus on the delay? Pull over to assist a stranded driver if you see that their car has broken down or they have a flat tire, rather than curse the traffic disturbance or drive on by. I bet that if you were in trouble you'd appreciate a helping hand, a kind word, or use of a cell phone to call work to advise them you'll be slightly detained or to call for a tow-truck. Part of who you are and how you show up in the world includes how you conduct yourself while operating any type of vehicle. A very wise matriarch in my life once suggested: "Pay attention to how people drive and how they conduct themselves in traffic. This will speak volumes to you of the character of this individual. If they will tell off complete strangers, and treat others flippantly and impatiently with slander and disrespect, they will do the same to you! Choose your associates, friends, and business partners wisely."

Example – desperation mirror

I had the privilege of experiencing many desperation mirrors with regard to being desperate for a relationship because of the fear of being alone. I was fearful of being with myself because I had not yet learned how to love and enjoy my own company. In my socialization I learned that love was external to me rather than within me. I believed I needed someone else to love me because I did not know how to love myself. When I truthfully acknowledged that this neediness repulsed me, I understood it. This explained how I set myself up to be rejected by others when I exhibit this same behavior. This check-up from the neck upwards provided opportunity for me to get to know myself, to learn new ways of being available to myself. It is a gift to be vulnerable first with myself, to acknowledge my thoughts, feelings, actions, and to own my relationship results. My needs are valid and they are not repulsive. It provided opportunity for me to ask myself, "What do I need? What do I want? How can I best meet my needs and wants?" I began to explore how to meet my "tenderness and touch needs," by going for a massage or swimming. I began to meet my need for companionship by volunteering, organizing entertainment activities with friends, taking general interest classes to meet new people, and going out to dances. I began to do things on my own rather than wait for someone to go with me to movies, hiking, walking, and weekend getaways. I have come a long way in developing a relationship with my self, and now, when someone asks me if I am single, I have heard myself respond, "Yes, I live with myself and I love the company."

I can say that now, however, I have had many relationships and two marriage experiences. In one case I partnered with a really laid-back man, at a time when I was not able to express that in my life. I was goal-oriented, driven to achieve, to do, to climb the corporate ladder, to be somebody, because I believed I had to earn my value. All the while he was showing me to be content, go with the flow, relax, and be. This relationship dissolved and, thankfully, I am learning to effect a wholesome, fulfilling balance with regard to doing and being.

A decade later, I partnered with someone the polar opposite of my first marriage companion. This was fueled by a limiting belief I had, which said, " I just have to settle down and be married by the time I'm thirty!"

I was so caught up in creating the "dream wedding" that the reality of marriage relationship that comes after the wedding did not receive due consideration. The excitement energy of the dream over ruled my logic, even though a couple of folks asked me:

"Do you know what you are doing?"

Chances are with the divorce statistics what they are, I'm not the only person to experience the consequences of rushing into a marriage in order to live the dream wedding.

I'm not proud of my hindsight in my desperation and investment in the idea of being married by a certain age. I admitted to myself that I was in love with the idea of being married, rather than with the man I agreed to marry. Although, the season of our soul interaction was not a lifetime commitment, lives were transformed positively by the union.

In my case I experienced the extremes in marriage mates, and now I am learning, by choice, to live in a wholesome, balanced manner without an attachment to someone else.

How can I be patient, compassionate, forgiving, tolerant, understanding, appreciative, accepting, and loving in a relationship with another, unless I have experienced it by giving it to myself?

Example – "life happens to me rather than through me" mirror

There have been many folks in my life who served as teachers, providing examples of the "life happens to me" mirror. I had to admit that this powerful mirror was showing me how I waited for others to help me; how I even manipulated others to do things for me, rather than go out and take steps to promote myself, to get a job, and to make contacts.

When beginning an entrepreneurial venture I made up promotional material and expected others to promote me. I believed that others would provide publicity through a media release, others by referring friends to the website, and others distributing flyers detailing upcoming events. I really got the message when I repeatedly heard stories of various individuals applying for jobs through friends and not making any follow-up calls directly; not delivering their résumé in person, expecting others to do it for them and expecting to get the desired results. I finally told myself the truth of how this really perturbed me. Then I got the message in the mirror for myself – I have done exactly that in my life.

This turned me around the corner to being more proactive. Who can promote me better than I can? I asked for help through a community organization and learned how to effectively market myself professionally. Then I was hired to teach others how to market themselves effectively, which became my new career. I am not a piece of paper, an announcement, a flyer, a website, a business card, a résumé, or a professional profile. Like you, I am a living, inspiring force. Like you, I bring new perceptions, solutions, healing, hope, and service in a myriad of forms. Like you, I have developed a remarkable, transferable skill-set through my education, career, life, and voluntary service experience, which is of value and which enables one to make a significant and immediate positive contribution wherever you are in the moment.

Example – expectation mirror

I learned a new definition of expectation. I do not remember who to credit with sharing this idea with me: "Expectation is a premeditated resentment." The expectation mirrors in my life have been through the people closest to me in my personal and professional life. I have noticed that I am more tolerant, and have fewer expectations, of people I do not know very well. Interesting, isn't it, that when a stranger has to reschedule a get-together, I respond with "I understand," yet when someone close to me does it, I have been known to take it personally and hold a grudge. Admitting how often I had had plans and when something came up which appeared to be more appealing or all of a sudden became more of a priority, I called and rescheduled. It is interesting on this journey how quickly a life lesson is delivered. For me it transpired in a rapid succession of this type of mirror and I finally got the message. I've heard this saying many times: "The lesson will be repeated until you learn the lesson."

An aspect of the expectation mirror is keeping agreements. I was presented with the opportunity to ask myself, "How dependable am I? How good at keeping agreements am I? How could I possibly expect others to keep their word and follow through on their commitments if I did not?" I also learned that the most important individual for me to keep my agreements with was myself. I stopped abandoning myself. My new mantra became, "I will always be here for you, no matter what!"

In my experience, when my expectations are not met when I expect them to be, new relationship challenges are created. Unmet expectations create resentment and I have been know to exhibit a "keeping score" and a "give to get" mentality and at times a toxic "eye for an eye" behavior. Expectations create a subtle energy dynamic that has a detrimental effect on relationships. No one wins when this type of energy is running. Stopping the cycle takes plenty of perseverance, through the practice of self-observation and truth-telling.

What about the unspoken expectations that friends and family should do favors for free, yet when they are not available, the same services are contracted and paid for? This all revolves around expectation and an attachment to outcome – for example, asking a favor because I know the person or because they owe me one for having done something for them. This was a very uncomfortable mirror for me to look into. I had to come to terms with my "give to get" manipulation mentality. There was an undercurrent of expectation with regard to friends and family. I used duty, obligation, and guilt on someone to meet my present need, without consideration for what was going on in their lives. I needed help. I'd helped them. It was my turn to receive. I had many opportunities to practice freeing myself of these limiting thoughts and behaviors.

The complications in all of our relationship challenges are conflicting needs. They provide us with multiple chances to learn to live more compassionately. Rarely will we have the same thoughts, needs, emotional nature, psychological make-up, or spiritual understanding as the other person at the same time as they do. In our relationship endeavors, we are learning to give each other the benefit of an open heart, coherent with our open mind. Endeavor means to make a concerted effort. Concerted means together. Together we can learn and grow in relationships, and know and understand through experience. If, each time I connect with another person, I come with an open heart of reconciliation, energetically it sets the stage for a life-giving exchange. Plus, it is so wonderful to give each other the gift of listening. I love a message I received from a wise woman in my life: "If you are thinking while I am speaking, you have already interrupted me!" I was grateful for the gracious delivery of a message to make me conscious of my habit of interrupting others and jumping in to change the subject.

I remember a wonderful example of a dear soul mirroring compassion. A group of us went out of town for a New Year's Eve celebration. The significant other of this man pulled out of the group to be alone. It was clear that this individual was visibly and very obviously upset. This dear soul brother let his significant other have her alone time and when someone asked where his mate was responded, "Something must have triggered a past hurt. When she's ready to share, she will. She needs to be on her own just now and I respect that." He gave the gift of space. He put love first, and he did not take it personally. He did not do the self-centered thing and demand company because "after all, it was New Year's Eve." He demonstrated compassion, acceptance, understanding, and respect. I was so grateful to be a witness of the "care with passion" brand of compassion in action.

Example – office politics, gossip and dissention mirror

It's time to talk about the most prolific corporate parasite and relationship demolition force I have ever experienced. This is the office politics, gossip, and dissention mirror. I cannot count how many times I ran around this circle. I came by it honestly. I learned how to avoid conflict in my socialization and formal education, so I could now unlearn the avoidance. Given my history of limiting beliefs with regard to anger, you are probably not surprised. My past destructive habit was that when I had a grievance or difference of opinion, I would speak to others, hoping they would take it on and talk to the individual (play the co-dependent game). I have heard the notion that "dominant thought expands," so when I hold to the idea of being right and give it energy by repeating my story over and over, this is how it becomes the destructive dissention monster. The more I focus on an issue or an idiosyncrasy with regard to another, the bigger it becomes. Here are two sayings I have heard that put it succinctly: "Thoughts held in mind reproduce in kind" and "My dominant thoughts expand."

If instead I choose to value the other person by asking myself silently, "What is more important, the soul of _____ or this petty issue?" it puts things in perspective. Or what about making the choice to honor and have compassion for a friend or family member by being curious? Or how about asking myself silently, "I wonder what is going on in their life today? This is so out of character for them," before I react or judge harshly?

By speaking to everyone else rather than going directly to the person with whom I have a difference of opinion, I don't have to deal with my mistaken perception, my limited viewpoint, or take responsibility for my emotions. I could continue to delude myself that I was right.

I learned a concept from the Context Associated series of courses, that "explaining, complaining, and justifying are negative seductive strategies for being right. They are ways of getting behind my reasons, rather than owning and taking responsibility for my results." This type of behavior has also been called passive aggressive. On the surface you go along with the majority, but behind the scenes you try to convince others to see it your way. Or you silently go along in the moment and then later in public you voice your opinion as an attack or assault, perhaps humiliating or putting down the soul involved. Have you ever experienced or participated in this type of destructive behavior?

When I invested time and energy in self-study, I determined that being involved in this course of action allowed me to stay unconscious and I would resist having to learn what the particular situation was trying to teach me about me. For instance, I had to learn to take responsibility for my control issues. In my youth this served me very well to keep me safe. As an adult it became evident that my controlling was very annoying to others and created disharmony in relationships. What a relief to admit to myself that my belief in the need to be right was so destructive. How enlightening to learn that a right/wrong attitude and win/lose mentality are aspects of controlling. To be right, I would find fault, exploit weakness, and be an energy drain by withdrawing energy from the creative collective. It certainly continues to take practice to focus on the best in others, to motivate, inspire, encourage, and empower others to grow, by being nourishing rather than being toxic.

What became evident was that I was in the process of learning to accept my humanness. When I accept my humanness it enables me to believe that each soul does the best they know how to do with their current level of skill, ability, emotional state, and experience. Knowing that in order for me to give you the opportunity to be seen, heard, acknowledged, and validated, I must first learn to give this to myself. I recognize that as I affirm, value, and appreciate myself, as I respect and honor my feelings, I heal myself and create a life-giving relationship with myself. I now realize that the degree to which I experience healing within myself will equal the degree of healing in all my relationships because it ripples out to others.

I know of an organization that has made it a condition of employment to go directly to the person whenever you have an issue with an individual – it is grounds for dismissal when an individual talks about a person rather than to that person. In order for a policy of this nature to be effective, there needs to be a commitment agreement between all parties involved. There must be an individual commitment and daily practice by each member of the corporate echelon and staff team in order to effectively wipe out the office politics, gossip, and dissention parasites.

Example – controller mirror

Have you ever noticed, and been willing to admit to yourself, that you have controlling tendencies? I have had heaps of controlling mirrors in my life. I had to finally admit to myself what was underlying my control issues. In social situations I acknowledged an aspect of my controller as possessiveness. I realized through self-study that my suspiciousness and paranoia were symptoms of insecurity.

I also got to see, through many mirrors, how I would vie for attention by interrupting others who were speaking, so I could be more comfortable by controlling the conversation and being the centre of attention. This is when my need for acceptance, approval, and appreciation were high and I expected them to be met by people who were external to myself.

Also, I witnessed how, in strained group situations, I would withdraw my energy. I would not participate nor communicate when I wasn't in control. I exuded an "all or nothing" mentality. Silence, you see, is also another way to control.

There are billions of possible relationship mirrors available for us to practice with as we silently observe ourselves in our day-to-day interactions with others.

Closing remarks and exercise

I presented you with many examples from my personal experience of working with this technique. Your personal experience will be unique to you, because you and I have not had the same key relationships in life and do not have the same key relationships now, or the same professional relationships. Now you have a tool that you may utilize to become more conscious of your relationship interactions, if you desire to create and experience even more life-giving energy in them.

To start with, use this technique in your observation and in revealing the microscopic truth to yourself with regard to your five key relationships in life to date. This will give you plenty to practice and work with. When you complete those, move on to five key present relationships, and so on. I just know that the insights and consequential balancing of how you energetically express yourself in relationship with others will pay you lifelong dividends. Yes, you can create an aware, life-giving, loving relationship with yourself that will inevitably be reflected back to you through your relationship mirrors.

A wise patriarch in my life shared with me: "When you deal with seemingly difficult people, it's perhaps an opportunity for God to use them as sandpaper to smooth out your edges."

Together

Together we create,
A safe, sacred space.
To transcend our density,
Leaving not one trace.
With synergy of Spirit,
We raise our vibration.
And come to know energy,
Without limitation.

Terraced Hillside Experiences

Imagination exercise

As you make your departure from the mirrored cloud scenery, you stroll along the beach. Another ecosystem presents itself for you to explore as you continue the hike of life adventure. You see in the distance an incredible terraced hillside. The closer you get, the higher it appears to be. You notice that your strides are relaxed and you're walking with little or no effort. You are very conscious of your breath and how the wholeness of your being seems to be in synch. You are conscious of the natural rhythmic movement of your hips as they trace the infinity (figure-eight) symbol with each step. The hillside towers above you when you reach its base. Your naked eyesight is so clear, a consequence of revealing the truth to yourself and of your shifts in consciousness. Your awareness of self now shifts to a heightened awareness of your surroundings, and your heart stirs with these perceptions.

New perception

The hillside is symbolic of multiple levels of growth possibilities ahead of you. There are some soul brothers and sisters making their way along one of the terraced trails. Along the way you're sure to meet others who are balancing on life's ledges. We learn new skills, receive encouragement and allow support as we move through our lives. This affirms the truth that although your experiences are unique to you, you are not alone on your adventure of self-discovery and inner connection.

I had lived a couple of decades acknowledging only my physical and intellectual natures, but now my hike of my life adventure is showing me how to recognize my feeling nature and my spiritual nature. There is a connection between the thoughts I think, the feelings I have, and the action I take, and the results I experience as a consequence of them. My feeling nature is multifaceted. It also expresses in and through my body as well as through my emotions. I am learning that my body is a miraculous messenger that communicates with me very clearly. It is for me to learn to decode the messages it provides.

I am learning through practice how to develop a rapport relationship with the wholeness of my being. I can be conscious of the "psychology of selves" within me and live in a balanced, wholesome, harmonious manner with access to all aspects of my inner environment. Drs. Hal and Sidra Stone, in their book *Embracing Our Selves*, introduce the concept psychology of selves. They explain that within each of us is an entire family collective that creates our personality. Each aspect of self has a unique expression and, through their ground-breaking work, they share techniques to teach individuals to bring conscious awareness and understanding to the psychology of selves.

I have not arrived yet – "As long as I'm breathing, I'm learning." My life is a series of interactions with people, places, and things. When a present moment interaction triggers a past circumstance, it is an invitation for me to feel, deal, heal, and reveal truth to myself. I can silently ask myself, "Isn't this interesting? I'm curious about this stimulation. What is this trying to teach me about me? Obviously there is some residue from the past that needs to be acknowledged, or I would not have had my buttons pushed."

There is an aspect of myself that desires to be seen, heard, acknowledged, and validated by me. There is obviously some unfinished business from the past, perhaps unexpressed feelings, emotions that need to run their course, limiting beliefs to release, or worn out identities about myself that no longer serve me. Perhaps the question I need to ask myself is, "How far through the levels have I moved? Is there more of a clearing required? Have I got to the depth of my healing with regard to this issue?" Or you can say, "Here comes another one, an incremental step on my hike of my life adventure to response-able living!"

I can create support in my life by entering into a confidentiality agreement with an individual I meet along the way – a real-life skills coach, a spiritual advisor, a counselor, a therapist, a support group, or a medical professional. I realize that at times I need a witness so I can receive support and not be alone with my life experiences, dilemmas, or challenges. It is not a sign of weakness to seek, request, and receive help.

While journeying along this terraced hillside I can reach out to give and receive support. By that very act, I acknowledge my interdependence. The support we give and receive between each other is like extending a rope bridge that we can use to boost each other up to the next level of awareness and understanding. It is the encouragement that we offer each other to keep going and growing when the terrace feels like a valley.

On each terrace or plateau, I learn and practice new skills, and entertain new perceptions that empower me to make new choices and to experience new consequences. In moving through a trauma of my life experience there are a number of incremental terraces. The first is playing the victim role and its consequences, followed by the survivor role part of the process. Then there is a decision to venture forth and be a thriving individual, and finally to reap the rewards of being victorious in the victor role. Each is unique and is an essential part of the process of feeling, dealing, and healing by revealing the truth of my personal past to myself. It is a moment-by-moment choice to participate fully in my own life by creating and thriving rather than just coping and surviving.

Foundation terrace – a story

A soul sister shared a story with me about her daughter. One day the little soul packed her wee tote bag and announced to her mom that she was leaving. Before she left she came to give her mom a hug, which was their ritual each time they departed each other's company. Her mom asked, "Where are you going?" The wee soul responded, "I'm going to live in the grocery store." To which the mother replied, "Oh, does this mean you're running away?" Then the daughter asked, "Didn't you ever run away?" Mom said, "No."

Perplexed, the daughter asked, "Didn't you ever wanna run away?" Mom said, "Yes, lots of times. Come here!" As she motioned to her daughter she patted the carpeted floor beside her. "Let's sit down on the floor and talk about this." The daughter obliged her mom and sat clutching her wee tote bag.

Mom: "I wanted to run away a lot, but this one thing I knew. If I run away from my problem, it will never get solved. It will just follow me and go with me wherever I go. I have learned that I have to sit down right in the middle of my problem and observe it from all angles and wait for an idea. When I get an idea, I put it into practice and give it a go. If it doesn't work, I go back and sit down in the middle of the problem again. I look at it again and I even ask for help from others because they may see the problem differently. Then I sit down again and I wait for an idea. That's how I solve the problem. Then there is no more problem and I don't have to run away."

You can use the wisdom from such a simple story to assist you when facing your life challenges and problems. This story affirmed for me that dealing with difficulties is indeed a process. It's not a matter of making one change and, hey presto, no more difficulty. I approached the terraced hillside portion of the hike of my life adventure with addiction as my number one priority. Therefore, addiction will be the first topic of discussion. Addiction, as defined in *Webster's II New Riverside Edition*: "to surrender (oneself) habitually or compulsively to something, such as caffeine or alcohol."

What I now know to be true through self-study is that I was not only addicted to certain substances but I was addicted to certain ways of thinking and behaving in endeavoring to meet my needs, albeit destructively. For me the forms of addiction have changed over the years, and each form was an integral part of a miraculous transformation from self-loathing to self-loving.

Terrace of self-worth

I invite you into the process of my limited self-worth condition. I was addicted to achieving and doing. I tried to earn or buy my self-worth and self-esteem. Have you ever felt empty? Have you experienced an insatiable longing? Have you ever wondered when you'll feel satisfaction and fulfillment? You're not alone. Have you experienced numerous relationships, careers, travels, possessions, achievements, and have still not been able to satisfy the longing or fill the empty void? The bad news is that you will never fill the void through outer distractions, outer correction, or by changing your external environment. The good news is that the longing is a call from your spiritual nature for conscious acknowledgment. Conscious, as defined in *Webster's II New Riverside Edition*: "aware of one's own existence, sensations, and environment; capable of thought, will, or perception; awake and deliberate." It is possible to fulfill the need and satisfy the longing through inner connection. Hopefully, within the energy of these pages you will find for yourself ideas that resonate with you and will assist you in exploring your sacred inner environment.

John S. Powell, in his book *Happiness is an Inside Job,*

relates a story about a time when he was preparing to give a talk and he was curious about his level of nervousness. When he paused for silent reflection and prayer, he perceived a message that came through his open heart and mind from the divine: "Stop performing so others see how great you are and start loving, so others see how great they are." This was inspiration for me to stop being so self-serving and self-centered. It really showed me how my performing was a desperate call for acceptance, approval, and recognition from outside myself.

When I practice accepting and giving myself the "care with passion" brand of compassion, I can practice doing the same for others. In order to start loving so that others see how great they are, I needed to experience it first-hand. In my life I heard many times, and intellectually knew, the biblical commandment written in the book of Leviticus 19:18 – "love your neighbor as yourself." There is a great difference between knowing something and learning something through experience. This is when the knowledge becomes wisdom. It was clear to me that I was being called to learn, practice, and live it.

Exercise

Here is an invitation for you to do an invaluable inventory process. This is your opportunity to determine and clearly identify for yourself: "What is my self-worth attached to?"

"Self-worth = net worth" was a limiting belief which I faced on the self-worth terrace. I had to let go of what the world of banks call my net worth. When I was turned down for a loan to purchase a vehicle upon my return from my world pilgrimage, I went through an identity crisis. My self-esteem was attached to the mistaken identity that, to be successful, I had to prove or earn my self-worth by having material wealth. I realized that this limiting belief was what caused me to feel devastated when I was declined a loan by the bank. After all, I had bought my first overseas trip at age fifteen, my first automobile at sixteen, and my first home at nineteen. I had borrowed and paid out numerous mortgages and loans. The challenge or opportunity of this circumstance was for me to let go of the limiting belief that net worth and self-worth were one and the same. It was obvious that this belief no longer served me.

I am wealthy. My life is richer and more meaning-filled because of the treasure that I perceive I am in truth, and the rich value I appreciate expressing through all that is a part of my life. Now let's introduce the exercise.

Part A

I invite you to make a list of all the achievements that are attached to your self-worth. This is a process I learned during my research and I cannot remember who to credit. In my eagerness to do the exercise, I neglected to note in my journal the name of the individual who shared this inspirational concept. However, I believe it to be incredibly valuable. This is how I wrote it in my journal and I share the process with you. This will probably take more than a few minutes. Use a fresh sheet of paper or clean page in a journal and as things come to mind note them and keep adding to your list over the course of days, weeks, or months. Each time you identify something outside yourself which you acknowledge for yourself that your self-worth is attached to, make an entry on the list. That is the first step. The second step is to say aloud to yourself in a mirror, if you have one, "I now affirm that I have value, regardless of _____ [fill in the blank with the achievement or external item]." Take the time to do this and you will be amazed. Be thorough and be willing to tell yourself the microscopic truth.

Part B

Make a list of what you have perceived to be the bad things you have done up until now. Be thorough and be willing to really search yourself for all the truth. Each time you make an entry on this list, affirm out loud, "I now affirm I have value, regardless of my achievements and regardless of _____ [fill in the blank with the perceived bad thing you have done]." Remember the power of three – think it, say it, and hear it.

Part C

The next part is to create a list of what you have perceived to be the times when your essence was not in truth honored by those about you. Each time you write something, affirm out loud, "I now affirm I have value, regardless of my achievements and regardless of the perceived bad things I have done, and regardless of _____ [fill in the blank with the perceived bad thing that was done to you], and so it is for all others."

Then comes the grand finale to this exercise – pray. Here is an example of a possible prayer.

"Holy Spirit, I willingly surrender my entire inventory list of attachments. This is not the truth of who, and whose, I am. I release, I let go, I let God heal me at depth. Create in me a new room for limitless love of self and others. I open to receive and accept miraculous healing, new perceptions, in the name and through the power of the living Christ presence. I give thanks for all of life and so it is. Amen. Thank you God."

I say "possible" prayer because I encourage you not to limit yourself using this prayer. Be spontaneous and pray as your intuition guides you in connecting with the God of your understanding. There are innumerable ways to make a divine connection.

Having completed this exercise for myself, did I have it handled, once and for all? No, there are, and will continue to be, times when I need to remind myself of this valuable exercise, because I'm still living, moving, and breathing in my experience of life. This modus operandi distinctly showed me how I had attached my identity and value to people, places, and things outside of me, rather than making the inner connection to know and understand the truth of my innate divinity.

When I asked Spirit for a miraculous, new, healed perception, I got it. The mantra I received was "I am a miracle," and so it is with you. You are a beloved, precious miracle!

Terrace of compulsive-addictive behavior

My addictions served me in a number of ways. First, when I wanted to feel something other than emotional pain I would distract myself by doing something. What I learned was that the emotional need or desire, my feeling nature, was very strong and this would override my logical mind. Many times, I would do something because I wanted to feel pleasure. I would meet the need without stopping to think about the consequences, because the power of the emotion overruled my logic every time.

The flip-side of this coin was that when I felt badly and did not want to feel that way any longer, again I looked outside myself for relief. I used things to medicate, numb, or busy myself to avoid painful emotions. Unfortunately, this gave only temporary relief and when the trauma within grew in strength and intensified it would fuel a huge surge of compulsive-addictive behavior. You may identify in the following list some familiar coping strategies that you employ: a binge eating episode, a binge smoking and drinking episode (to black out), a drunken binge sex episode (string of one-night stands), a binge work episode (to exhaustion so I could sleep), a binge spending episode (credit card debt), a binge isolation reading education episode, a binge vacation (credit card debt), a binge physical fitness regime, a binge entertaining flurry, a binge prescription drug episode to sleep through weekends, a binge on spiritual materialism or a binge on voluntary service – and the list quite possibly could be endless.

This craziness did serve a purpose for me. By asking myself these questions, I was able to begin to unravel complex issues and consciously work through them.

"What do I really need?"

"What do I truly want to experience?"

"What do I crave to feel?"

"What am I trying to avoid feeling?"

"How can I creatively meet this need, experience these feelings, and satisfy these emotions in new and different ways?"

"How can I shift this destructive habit into constructive life-giving habit?"

"What resources are available in the community to give myself the gift of support?"

I am so grateful that with plenty of support I have successfully freed myself from addictions to prescription pain medication, alcohol, nicotine, caffeine, and over – spending. I have learned over the years that the crutch changed form and I am hope-filled that in time, I will no longer need a crutch at all.

I received support with regard to binge disordered eating behaviour. The truth is, I used food to medicate, to numb, so I could postpone or even avoid feeling.

Plus, I acknowledged that it was the only response my upset wounded inner child was familiar with – food. Although, I am a grown woman it became evident that it was the impulse of my wounded child that was unconsciously running the show. Once I became aware, I could change this energy pattern.

The actionable steps I took included purifying my nutrition plan by removing stimulants. I sought counseling so I could have a witness for the emotional pain of my wounded child. I began to develop a new life – giving relationship with my physical body through the practice of meditation and conscious breath work.

It was the conscious breath work that empowered me to locate emotional congestion I had stored in my physicality when I brought my conscious awareness to a congestion using focused breath work, an energy release transpired. I would release the unexpressed emotion, usually in the form of crying and tears. I made time to facilitate this process and allow the emotions to run their course. My extra weighte-dress my armour of protection began to melt away as I was willing to feel, deal and heal.

It is so empowering to realize I can correct my compul-sive addictive disordered eating behavior. I can use food for its true purpose of sustenance. My body responded well and in time I became aware of and experienced true physical hunger. At mealtime I chose to eat food for energetic vitality. I gave up my habit of eating between meals and chose to drink water instead.

I concluded food has served me well in the sense that it satisfies so many of my needs and wants. However, my destructive compulsive behavior has created too much weight upon my physical frame and this creates health risks. I identified how food serves me: as an instant gratification or distraction; as comfort, pleasure, and a way of loving myself; as suppressant medication to numb and provide temporary relief to avoid feeling; as celebration; as a treat or reward; as punishment when I feel feelings which, up until now, I judged as unacceptable; and as nourishment, which is the true purpose of food.

How do your addictions serve you?

It is important to identify how the addiction serves you before you can make lasting changes. The addiction does not drive you. It is the pay-off or the emotional need that the addiction fulfills that fuels the addiction and makes it a driving force of control over your intellect.

As a youngster I learned that my emotions, or my expression of emotions other than happiness, was unacceptable. The adults in my life rarely gave permission for me to express my feelings freely and naturally. It also occurred to me that, even though the adults in my life during my childhood did not give me permission to express myself, I did not have to perpetuate this learned habit of abandoning myself.

While visiting this terrace, I began to observe how children have little temper tantrums that naturally last about three to four minutes. In my youth I had adopted a limiting belief that being emotional was not good. Then, of course, if one is punished for being emotional, you adopt the limiting belief that feelings are wrong. A couple of gifts I received on this terrace were from my observation of children. I opened my mind to admit to myself that I learn from people of any age. I willingly surrendered the limiting belief that teachers must be older than me. The truth is that we are all teachers of, and learners from, each other.

Example – children as teachers

I was relaxing on a lounge chair on a sandy beach at a local park, enjoying the sea breeze and the sun dancing and sparkling on the water surface, when two figures caught my attention. These two young boys were building a sandcastle. They appeared to be having words and the larger of the two boys ordered the younger boy to go get a bucket of water from the sea. The little person stood, put his hands on his hips, frowned, and then grabbed the bucket and stomped down to the water. The other boy stood up and pounced on and flattened the portion of the castle that the younger boy had been molding and shaping. When the younger, smaller boy returned with the bit of water that had not sloshed out of the bucket, he was shocked to see his part of the castle crumpled. He shoved the shoulder of the older boy, who was squatting, and he tumbled over. They had a bit of a scrimmage that lasted a couple of minutes, and then they rolled around laughing together. They jumped up, turned their attention back to the sand, and started working together on a new creation. This was marvelous for me to witness. Promptly air your differences, express yourself without harming anyone, laugh together, roll out and then let go of the differences, and then together get back on track and create something totally new and different for the highest good of all. Thank you boys for being such a great demonstration for us all.

My destructive compulsive-addictive behavior with regard to my emotional nature was that I would feed my feelings. I would stuff them down. I would be nice, nice, nice on the surface, when inside I was full of frustration at not knowing how to express myself. Repetition of this habit created thoughts of resentment and anger that I chewed over and over again. This dynamic built more pressure and I became afraid to express myself, which created anxiety. That was, until I experienced an emotional breakdown to breakthrough. I couldn't control my feelings and emotions any longer. This was a very positive force. However, at the time it was extremely intense. I highly recommend that you honor your feeling nature by constructively expressing your emotions rather than denying them.

In the movie *Tuesdays With Morrie,* Jack Lemmon's character said, "How can you spare someone's feelings by denying them?" This really touched the heart of truth within me. When I thought about this from a victim mindset, I easily acknowledged that I have had dear souls in my life who believed it was okay for them to say what they felt and to experience their emotions. I had learned in my socialization that it was inappropriate for me to do the same. I was repeatedly hushed and ordered: "Don't say anything to upset _____."

From a response-able mindset, I decided I would no longer betray and abandon myself by denying my own feelings. I finally believed that my feelings were valid. Even if and when others did not think so, I could still be available to myself. This doesn't mean I spout off whatever is on my mind and tell others off all the time. It means that I validate what and how I am feeling when I am feeling it, rather than repress, suppress, or resist feeling. What do I mean by resisting my feelings? Have you ever been emotionally stimulated and got busy to distract yourself from feeling? Have you ever phoned up someone and made plans to do something to avoid dealing with how you were feeling? Have you ever lost yourself in fantasy thoughts about "someday isle" by letting yourself become consumed with planning for the future or wondering what it will be like when…? I realized in time that these were all the compulsive-obsessive and addictive behaviors I employed to resist feeling and to resist change.

They kept me very busy, busy, busy in my head and it finally became evident to me that this habit pattern no longer served me.

When I practice being available to myself by honoring and respecting my feelings, I am able to do the same for others. How can you possibly take a step of vulnerability with anyone, unless you first take a step of vulnerability with yourself?

Terrace of acceptance

One aspect of dealing effectively with an addiction is the concept of acceptance. It is important to begin to accept all of your feelings and admit to yourself that you have self-defeating thoughts. There is a valuable quote I heard, which I paraphrase in first person: "Whatever I resist will persist until I deal with it." This means that when you attempt to push away whatever it is you are thinking, feeling, or struggling with, you give it more power and it grows stronger. If, on the other hand, you accept your thoughts and feelings as part of your humanness, then they lose the power to control you and to lead you into compulsive-addictive destructive behavior. Here are some tools that may assist you when observing and learning to own and take responsibility for your thoughts.

Exercise

In the silent observation of your own thoughts, you catch yourself on an anxiety tangent over something or someone.

To demonstrate the concept, let's use anxiety in this example. Say out loud or silently to yourself when you catch yourself thinking compulsive-obsessive thoughts, "Okay, _____ [fill in the blank with a word that adequately describes your thought and consequential feeling]. Anxiety, I know you. I recognize you. I acknowledge you. I accept you. I am conscious of you. You are not in control of me any more, Spirit is." Then place your hand on your heart and continue to repeat this sentence or one that suits you, to yourself until you feel that you are calm, centered, and grounded.

Will you do this once and never be plagued by anxiety again? I don't think so. I know for myself that I use this technique over and over again so that I am not at the mercy of my thoughts. I repeat it each time I catch myself leaking energy away from the life-giving present moment. If I'm fretting about the future, or fuming over the past, I am very definitely in my head and separating myself from the present moment.

In addition, to anchor yourself in the power-filled present moment, focus on something you appreciate. A quick way to accomplish this is to focus on and acknowledge something in your immediate environment that is a gift from one of your five senses. What is there for you to appreciate through the gift of your sight, smell, taste, hearing, or touch? In conclusion, engage your brain by creating and affirming an appreciation, a gratitude, or a truth. This technique is to fill in the void where the anxiety thought used to be. If you do not choose a different thought, it will come back again and you continue your practice until you are no longer anxious. The possibilities are endless and your creativity will surprise you once you provide opportunity for it to express itself.

My old destructive way of pushing away certain thoughts and feelings was a learned destructive habitual way of living.

As I worked with this technique, I created a page in my journal to note the different thoughts, feelings, or aspects of self that I was finally accepting and which previously would unconsciously and destructively control me. My list is rather lengthy – however, it may assist you in understanding the versatility of this technique.

Here is a list of the words I identified during my compulsive-obsessive thoughts self-study observation process: worry, fear, judgment, criticism, indecision, inner criticism, envy, jealousy, separation, gossip, aggravation, defensiveness, revenge, stubbornness, defiance, insensitivity, hypocrisy, isolation, embarrassment, an eye for an eye, resentment, expectation, fantasy, victim behavior, shame, guilt, pain, belief in lack, procrastination, attention grabbing, neediness, bitterness, self - consciousness, fault finding, condescension, attacking, blaming, caretaking, enabling, competitiveness, knowing it all, maliciousness, passive-aggressive behavior, paranoid fantasy, doing, pleasing, attachment to outcome, control, all or nothing, co-dependence, and win/lose.

Exercise

Then I received inspiration to create a song to sing in order to affirm, accept, and validate various aspects of myself: "Lorill, Lorill, Lorill, I love you, love you, love you, _____ you" [I filled in the blank to make "anxious you," "worrier you," "judgmental you," etc.]. All these words described an aspect of my human experience and I was learning how to honor, respect, and accept my humanness. When I do this for myself then I can do it for others, and so it is with you.

For a time, I incorporated this little singing technique while commuting in the car. What a life-giving way to use my energy while I sat in traffic. Rather than fuming and worrying and getting caught up in the situation, I sang. I was learning through experience what I heard on an audio cassette by Louise L. Hay: "Love is always the answer to healing of any sort."

You can silently use this technique when using public transport, and arrive at work with a smile on your face, a bounce in your step, and joy in your heart. Enthusiasm for life is contagious, and when someone is in the vicinity of your delight-filled energy, you make a difference.

Here are more items that were added to the list. You'll notice that the following are more positive characteristics, qualities, or adjectives that best describe aspects of self that I felt inspired to acknowledge and accept: appreciative, trusting, spontaneous, responsible, joyous, gentle, goodness, kindness, risk-taking, creative, willing, sensitive, generous, inspiring, growing, compassionate, playful, open, hope-filled, listener, teacher, encouraging, musical, adventurer, Goddess, perceptive, earth angel, Aphrodite, shy, deter-mined, authentic, communicator, instinctive, intuitive, mother of invention, and so on. I'm sure you've got the idea by now.

You may be inspired to make a customized audio cassette recording to listen to rather than read from a list, and you can privately do your self-acceptance exercise any time, any place, anywhere, using a Walkman. Get ready to witness a miraculous transformation in the relationship with yourself that will be life-giving to you and ripple outward to all with whom you interact. You will amaze yourself as you become more tolerant, accepting, and compassionate of others.

Another idea is that you might like to give a very personal gift to someone. Make a customized audio cassette recording of you speaking or singing acceptance of all these aspects using the name of the individual you're giving the cassette to. When I did this on several occasions it was very well received. Incidentally, when I did create an audio recording, I alternately used one characteristic from each list so that it was well balanced.

I had read the biblical verse I Corinthians 13:13, "faith, hope, and love, these three; but the greatest of these is love." I was now experiencing the healing balm of love and acceptance in my own life and it was finally beginning to make sense. Intellectual knowledge became wisdom through experience.

While we're on the topic of love, here's a question for you. How many are involved in a love relationship? When I was initially asked this question during an experiential course, I answered "one," and that was seven years ago. Now I am practicing this. I would like to share a personal example of what I mean by this. During a retreat weekend I met a very interesting and talented soul brother. We walked together, talked, held hands, and there was this lovely chemistry between us. Then the day ended and the next day was different. He decided it important I know that he had a "lady friend," but I still had the memory of the spontaneous play and fun that contributed to a wonder-filled day. I did acknowledge to myself my disappointment because he was not available for a relationship with me on a long-term basis. I had felt this way in the past – I had robbed myself of the joy of the moment by wishing things were different than they were, robbed myself of the joy of having a male platonic friend. In the past I would escape to fantasy because I did not like, or was not willing to accept, the reality of the current circumstance. I was not willing to face my feelings and deal with them as I was feeling them.

I paused and during a quiet meditation time silently asked God, "What is my lesson in this relationship interaction? The answer I perceived from this open receptive state was remarkable: "You have just experienced the feeling of excitement in connection with someone outside of yourself. Now have a different experience, without the attachment to a person, place, or thing external to yourself." "Okay," I said, "I'll just sit here in silence until I make the inner connection to the degree that I had made the outer connection."

When I sat in silence and focused on my heart, which I consider to be the divine connection to Spirit, I felt the Holy Spirit Rush. In the past when things did not turn out the way I had hoped or when relationships came to an end, I would become depressed for days, weeks, and sometimes months. On this occasion it was a matter of hours. I believe in miracles. I may not have walked on water, but I walked out of a hole before it became a huge valley. That's what you'll find on the hike of life adventure. You will experience your growth by the difference in your responses to circumstances as you journey.

Terrace of forgiveness

Another terrace on the healing path of addiction is forgiveness. When I heard *Heartmath*'s version of forgiveness – "love is for giving" – it resonated with me and I began to weave it into the fabric of my own life. My forgiveness of self dialogue went something like this: "Lorill, please forgive me for entertaining separation thoughts and giving free rein in my mind to judgment, criticism, and condemnation. Forgive me for perceiving and looking at you through the contaminated lens of conditional love attached to my past hurts. Forgive me for putting you in a prison of your past unconscious mistakes, acting-out behaviors, and unskilled behaviors. Forgive me for taking others prisoner and attempting to make them responsible for your pain. I'm so sorry for the abuses that happened to you in your very young years. It is not your fault."

The gift of this simple exercise had a profound implication, which I will present to you in the form of a question: how can I possibly perceive or see another as innocent with unskilled and acting-out behaviors unless I first perceive or see myself as such?

I invite you to ponder a new perception of forgiveness, an excerpt from my journal:

"I am not the enemy, you are not the enemy. The enemy is the wounds (the thoughts) within each of us that continue to bleed (contaminate) and destroy our hearts longing for life-giving, loving, respectful, honoring relationships. I must first begin by being available to myself. Allow all aspects of myself to tell me the true story of the life they lived and experienced. I hereby commit to feeling, dealing, and healing my wounds and to stop making others prisoners of my unresolved pain, my suppressed unhealed emotions, and my woundedness."

Following is an example of one of my journal entries. When I asked in prayer for help to redefine forgiveness from a soul perspective, this was the result. I realize that this is not grammatically correct, but it is the language of the heart, not the intellect.

> "Dear soul, _____. No matter what you have said, done, thought in the past, through unconscious and unskilled behavior; no matter what you will say, do, or think in the future; no matter your present judgments, perceptions, grievances, projected feelings, beliefs, or limitations; I am willing to acknowledge the me that is of God and I acknowledge the part of you that is of God. There is no separation. We are a miraculous powerful experience of the energy of love. God creates a new beginning for us from this moment on and there is freedom to be."

Have you ever heard or seen the word "Namaste?" I have a framed print of one of the definitions, signed by Ingrid Paterson in 1988, which says: "I honor the place in you in which the entire universe dwells. I honor the place in you that is of light, of love, and of truth. When I am in this place in me and you are in this place in you, we are one." When I journeyed to India and Nepal I witnessed people greeting each other in this manner. They would place their hands palms together with all their fingers pointing upward and holding their hands at their heart as they bent slowly forward in the direction of the individual they were greeting. What a beautiful, gentle manner in which to honor and greet each other.

When you endeavor to keep your heart open to those about you, silently affirm to yourself: "Namaste, a simple word to say, feel its meaning in your heart today!" Incidentally, this was a mantra I'd sing occasionally in the car during my commute. A hope-filled way to set the stage for a busy workday with those who I found challenging in the workplace. Enjoy the results you get by approaching others with an open heart of reconciliation and forgiveness in lieu of the habitual need to be right, fueled by superiority, condemnation, blame, resentment, and anger.

Exercise – verbal forgiveness

During a forgiveness workshop, we were asked to form diads (groups of two) where we sat on chairs facing each other with our knees almost touching. We were asked to repeat the following exercise three times for each issue. An added note is that when working with a particular issue, you may have more than one individual to name in the exercise. It is extremely important to work with one individual at a time.

The person I need to forgive is _____ [name].
I forgive you for _____ [issue].
I would have preferred that _____.
I accept you as you are.
I accept myself as I am.
So, _____ [name],
I forgive you,
I release you,
I let you go.

I behold the God in you.
I am free.
You are free.
From this place, I send you love.
Thank you, I set you free.

Repeat this three times.

Do you do this dialogue for an individual once and you've got it handled? Ha, ha, ha, I don't think so. However, it tills the soil from which your forgiveness work will blossom and grow.

It is of the utmost importance that you forgive yourself each time you experience a recall of a past circumstance when you were less than pleased by your own thoughts, words, deeds, or actions. Rather than push away the embarrassing memory, you allow it to come forward. You acknowledge your own humanness. You accept the circumstance as part of your life experience, knowing that all you have in life is your experiences. You carry on a dialogue silently with yourself and say, "_____ [fill in the blank with your name or nickname at the time], I forgive you. I accept you. I release you from my own judgmental, critical, and self-condemning thoughts. You are free. I love you completely, even this part that was involved in this act or this scene from my past. I need the energy of you in present-day time with me now, not frozen in the past."

This is only a suggested dialogue. You will more likely be inspired with your own words that flow through your own heart of truth to nourish, bless, and free you from the trap of your own "unforgiveness."

Exercise – written release regarding strained or estranged relationship challenge

This example is the language of the heart as it flowed for me and is not intended to be a grammatically correct paragraph.

> "Thank you for the gift of your presence in my life. My life is richer and more meaning-filled because of the treasure of you. Although for a short season the profoundly powerful mirror that you were for me showered me with blessings to learn and grow. Life is consciousness as we know, however, experiencing our consequence of our consciousness is the truth of our spiritual quest. Too often, I take people, places, possessions and positions and life itself for granted. I am so grateful and choose to be appreciative for all my life experiences and that of course includes my experience of you and our shared spiritual evolution. I see radiant, vital health, life-giving relationships, and fulfillment for you. From *Heartmath* I learned: "Love is for giving. I open to beam you love, rather than contract and deny us both. Namaste, dear heart _____.""

In time I was able to follow through and actually write and send this to others in homemade greeting cards and to be in integrity with myself. Forgiveness cannot be forged or forced – it is indeed a process that will evolve as you are willing to feel, deal, heal, and reveal to yourself the microscopic truth.

Exercise – creative visualization forgiveness

Have you ever gazed lovingly and appreciatively at a person, place, or thing? Have you ever attempted to gaze lovingly and appreciatively at yourself in the mirror?

Sit in a comfortable position on a chair or on the floor, facing a mirror. Look into your eyes. Allow your eyes to go out of focus. Focus and gaze at yourself in the mirror and breathe into your heart. Take in a few long slow inhalations and exhalations. Now envision your innerlight within your own heart and imagine you are beaming love to the image of yourself in the mirror. Continue to do this and the beam gets stronger and stronger. Allow yourself to receive this subtle, delicate, yet powerful, love energy.

As you sit in silence facing yourself and beaming yourself light and love energy, an aspect of self may object, believing that because of all that you have done up until now in your life, you are not worthy. Love is for giving. You give up each limiting belief as it comes forward to you for love. You may experience a cloud-like haze developing between you and the image of you in the mirror. This is palpable and visible energy of unconditional love. Bask in it and enjoy it.

Personal experience

A whole new process evolved for me as a result of practicing this technique. When I first did this exercise, I was extremely tearful. Afterward, in prayer, I asked: "Why my tears? What are the tears trying to teach me?" My answer was: "You have not forgiven yourself and you carry much guilt energy. This dense guilt energy blocks your ability to perceive, receive, and believe that you are loving and loveable. You must be willing to acknowledge this guilt energy, then willingly surrender it for transformation."

As I was willing to acknowledge and accept my humanness, in my meditation practice I began to scan my life. During each session, scenes from the movie of my life would run through the projector of my mind and freeze-frame on a mistake. The scenes would be so clear. In the review of the situation or circumstance, I was able to identify guilt energy that had been projected upon me. In this process I was able to separate myself from the guilt energy that was not even my own but which I had adopted from someone else. I envisioned each ball of guilt energy in my mind and with an abrupt exhalation pretended to blow it into white light. As the process evolved I was accountable to myself and owned my role in each scene. I also acknowledged that I did my best with my level of skill and ability at the time. I prayed for assistance and by the grace of God I continue this ongoing practice whenever more guilt surfaces for me to deal with in this constructive manner.

Years later there evolved more on forgiveness. Heading south of the border for a weekend getaway, I journeyed on my own by car for six hours. I was extremely pensive and in the quiet hours scenes from my life and individuals came to my conscious awareness. Individuals with whom I was still harboring ill will. As each individual and scene came forward, I would freeze the situation and envision myself saying directly to them, " _____ [fill in the blank with their name], I forgive you, I release you, and I let you go. Please forgive me, release me, and let me go." I arrived at my destination just on time to participate in a special meditation service in preparation for Easter.

The following day, while standing on a bridge that crossed a stream, a dear soul sister guided me through a process. She encouraged me to face downstream and release what I identified no longer served me. In my mind I silently said a prayer and asked for divine assistance to surrender and release what I most needed to be free of at this point in the spiritual evolution. Instantaneously came my answer: unforgiveness. I prayed: "Holy Spirit, I willingly surrender to you for miraculous healing of my unforgiveness toward myself and all others."

My friend intuitively knew when I was complete and invited me to turn upstream and open to receive what I most needed. I felt wave after wave of energy cascade over me and fill me. I experienced first-hand the powerful healing balm of unconditional love, a gift of grace, a symptom of forgiveness. I had finally surrendered the block within myself to my full experience of unconditional love. I gave up my unforgiveness and I am so grateful. I was moved to tears and unable to speak for some time for weeping.

My journey home was most interesting. The Easter Sunday service had allowed creative inspiration to flow through me in the form of a song: "Thank you God, expressing in, as, and through — [I initially used my own name and giggled with delight]." The very thought of acknowledging myself as a precious, beloved God-being tickled me. Did my intellect ever balk at the idea of not wanting to let go of the self-deprecating thoughts of: "Who, me? The unworthy one, the miserable sinner." I continued nonetheless, and then the name changed. Each scene and individual that had come forward to me on my outward-bound journey days earlier came forward for me to use in this song on my homeward-bound journey. I repeated the mantra, inserting their names, and it was significant indeed. At times I drove with tears streaming down my cheeks as I felt the unconditional love fill me and flow through me to each individual. I was surprised in many instances at not realizing there was still some residue to release from relationships that had ended two and three decades earlier. I am so grateful for this monumental growth spurt and consequential healing on my ever-evolving hike of my life adventure. Yeah, God!

Terrace of championing the critic

During my hike along the terraces of addictions, I walked and silently dialogued with my inner critic and asked for it to serve me in new ways. I wrote this in my journal: "Inner critic, thank you for all you have done to keep my child safe. What is important for you to know is that I am now an adult and I do not need protecting any longer. I would like us to come to a new agreement. I ask that you relax from your hyper-vigilant, controlling role and assume an assistant, discerning role so I can establish healthy boundaries for myself. I need your incredible attention to detail.

"I thank you for protecting me during my childhood. I am now an adult and I no longer need protecting. I wish to fully experience my heart in relationship with others. I'm learning to balance personal and impersonal energy in my personal and business relationships. For a full human life experience it is normal to include planned events and spontaneous events that honor and include my spiritual, emotional, physical, intellectual, psychological nature in a balanced, wholesome manner. You no longer have to run the show, simply participate. You're an integral part of my inner family, you're not dying. You're in safe hands. I care for and value your contribution in my life. I love you, inner critic, and I accept you. I listen for your assistance. I want you to know when I'm in a new job, new venture, or new relationship and I'm taking in a lot of new information. I am learning.

"I, like others, make mistakes and I learn from them. It's okay, inner critic – the world will not end. It's okay to relax and learn with me. I am living and learning moment by moment. Thank you, inner critic, for this new relationship with you."

Terrace of appreciation

In my mind I know that I require food as energy to fuel my body. When I ate unconsciously without stopping to give thanks for the food, I would eat for hours at a time and then sleep would follow because I had overtaxed my body. A step for me in learning to eat consciously was to incorporate a blessing over my meal before I ate. Not the traditional blessing which I have heard and said by rote for years on automatic pilot, but a heartfelt creative prayer that was unique to me. I share it with you with the intent that it may inspire you to give yourself permission to pray and give thanks in creative new ways.

"Thank you God for the gift of this energy. Thank you to all expressions of Spirit that participated in my receiving the gift of this energy. Thank you for blessing this energy to my body to create and maintain balanced, harmonious, radiant vital health and optimum well being. Bless me to your service for the highest good of all. Amen."

This is just one example and it is such a departure from the more conventional blessings. Spirit cannot be put in a box, for it is limitless. When others try to put me into a box, my spiritual being is not comfortable because the box is confining; it rubs, and chafes, and scrapes. We are free to commune with Spirit, the God of our understanding, in the manner that is best suited to us. I encourage you to give yourself permission to explore and have fun making your prayerful connections uniquely fulfilling.

When I was in public, at times I placed my hands over my food while silently praying a blessing over my meal. I had some servers ask me if my food was okay or if I was cold, because to them it appeared I was trying to warm my hands. In contrast, once while dining in an Indian restaurant, at the end of the meal I commented on how delicious the meal was and the server replied: "It was the prayer you said over the meal that made it taste so good." She would not take the credit – she gave the glory to the creator of all that is seen and unseen. What an awesome lesson in humility, delivered so graciously.

Terrace of more to life than me, me, me

What a revelation to wake up to the fact that the world does not revolve around me. The occasions are too numerous to mention here, of times when I went about pushing, doing, expecting others to assist me with meeting my immediate needs (when I wanted them met), while being totally unconscious and oblivious to the needs of others. The frustration that accompanied this limiting root core belief was a habitual way of being, which included frequent outbursts of impatience, reacting, tears, grumbling, complaining, attacking, and blaming, to name a few. "Me, me, me" is not a very honorable chant. I was blessed with many lessons through my personal and professional relationship interactions. They sure provided me with exceptional examples with which to work. I realized that a consequence of my abuse was that I had adopted the limiting belief that it is okay for people to take or get what they want and need, without consideration of the needs of others. It is natural for very young children to live within this behavioral pattern. However, I learned through numerous relationship experiences that it is not appropriate if I desire to create life-giving loving relationships as an adult.

If you desire to transform the me, me, me terrace experiences, I highly recommend including in silent thoughts and intentions the phrase "for the highest good of all concerned."

A personal story as example of me, me, me

Have you ever had an agreement to meet someone at a particular place, at a specific time, for an appointment, meeting, entertainment, or activity? Has the individual you were planning to meet with ever been late? What was your reaction? What were your thoughts? I have allowed time and lateness to really get the better of me. I used to nurse, curse, and rehearse how this person is frequently tardy, keeping me waiting, and I assumed that this meant that they did not respect me, and my mind would go and on and on. Here is one example of how I learned the benefit of relaxing and going with the flow rather than reacting and wasting and leaking my thought energy. Did I even pause to consider that they could have had an emergency at home, on the road, or a traffic accident that prevented them from being punctual?

One evening I was planning to meet a dear friend for a bike ride at a local scenic spot. The individual was fifteen minutes late and I was in reaction due to my choice to think unproductive thoughts. As it turned out, this individual stopped for some assistance with the bike rack that was used to transport my bike and her bike to our meeting place. She was concerned that the bikes would fall off and be damaged and that she would not make the trip because the bike rack was not fastening to secure the bikes as it was intended to do. I let go of my mini temper tantrum and we set off for a marvelous cycling experience along the dikes, with the mountains flanking us to the north, the farmers' fields to the south, and the dazzling brilliance of the setting sun directly in front of us. The super-scenic sights massaged my heart and soothed my soul, and I calmed down when I was in gratitude of the present moment and of the gift of the presence of this individual being with me to share the experience.

We stopped at a rest point for a drink of water and caught up on the time that had passed since our last visit. A spectacular light-show of yellow, gold, orange, red, and finally pink transpired. Wow! On our return trip we were blessed with the rising of a huge golden orange harvest moon trimmed in red. It was only visible for about fifteen minutes before slipping behind the dark clouds in the overcast eastern sky. Why do I share this story with you, when, had the individual been on time, we would have completely missed the moonrise? Things are not always what they seem on the outside at the onset. Sometimes missed appointments and accidents that initially are painful and challenging to us turn out to be a blessing in disguise. I am grateful how reaction on the me, me, me terrace transformed my impatience into a once-in-a-lifetime experience with an incredibly valuable life lesson. Not for just my good, but for the highest good of all.

You and I will not have identical terraced hillside experiences. In the discussion of the terraced hillside perception I have provided you with personal experiences and examples. Your own will evolve as you live the hike of life adventure. I encourage you not to limit your experience of working with these perceptions and ideas to only those presented in this treatise of pages. There are many colorful scenarios from your own life to interpret.

Let Us Reach Out and Give

Let us reach out and give.
Let us reach up and live.
Let us open to receive
The grace and courage to believe.
We are one heart, one mind.
Equal, so divine.
One heart.
One mind.
Universe.
Divine.

Waterfall Experiences

Congratulations for making your way along the many terraces and plateaus of the hillside hiking adventure. Once you make it to the top, pause and celebrate your increase in self-awareness and self-understanding. You are guided to make your way across this grand plateau to the edge of the cliff. You have walked a significant distance to be on the opposite side from where you initially stepped up off the terraces. You can hardly believe the glorious expanse before your eyes. To your amazement there is a waterfall vista that is absolutely breathtaking. Just look at the numerous waterfalls of varying heights, widths, and intensities. Take in a few long slow inhalations and exhalations, drink in the nurturing unconditional love that nature offers you. The sound of the water is deafening and yet the gentle mist is refreshing. The sparkling rainbow suspended in the sky truly is a symbol of hope as it twinkles in the sunlight. The multiple cascades of free-falling water are energy in motion.

Perception

I have heard emotions described as "e-motion – energy in motion." Are you, in this moment, ready to entertain a new perception of your emotional nature? Are you willing to consider that your emotions are energy in motion? They are the pureness of Spirit, moving naturally through your feeling nature. When your heart is touched, it opens from the connection with inspiration from limitless sources. Tears, when they flow naturally from our eyes, run down our cheeks and drop onto our chest, which houses our heart. The tears soften any hardness of heart and it becomes pliable and soft like clay. Relationships with self and others are transformed, and a new room is created for limitless unconditional love within the heart.

Perception explained

Let's assume for a moment that when you were young permission was not granted by those about you to express your emotional energy through your feeling nature. The energy of the emotion had to go somewhere. If it did not get expressed in the moment, you may have taken it out on someone else later, you may have drawn a disturbing picture at school, you may have acted out or suppressed it, storing the energy of the emotion internally, within your body. Imagine for a moment that each emotional expression is a grain of sand. Each time emotional energy is not expressed a grain of sand is stored within the body. When this action is repeated habitually, these grains of sand collect and create a density. Consider the possibility that when this density is concentrated into a congestion of stagnant emotional energy, it creates disease or discomfort in the physical body.

Just as there are multiple waterfalls in this vista before your eyes, there are multiple modes of expression for your emotionality. You can simply allow the emotion to run its course in the moment of awareness, feeling it, as children demonstrate to us so readily. You can journalize your feelings by writing them down when in private moments of self-awareness and reflection. You can speak on the phone to a noble friend, a trusted counselor, spiritual advisor, coach, teacher, or medical professional. You can speak your truth in a support group, spiritual community, club, or organization. You can facilitate the expression of your emotion through music, chanting, singing, or drumming. You can express yourself through the creation of poetry, songs, or short stories, creating characters to act out the drama or trauma that is wishing to express itself. You can use clay, pottery, pastels, pen and ink, watercolor, or oils to paint. You can work with material textures while sewing or stitching. You can facilitate yourself with movement, by attuning to your body in a new way. At other times you may feel compelled to move your body. Your body's innate wisdom may guide you to rock, roll, kick, bend, twist, make rapid movement, kneel, do circles, massage a particular part of your body, or combination of all of the above, which can evolve into a spontaneous dance.

You can draw from more familiar types of movement to determine which type of expression serves you best. You may choose to run, hike, swim, work with a ball, skip rope, punch a bag, golf, work with weights, ride a bike, or bounce on a trampoline or rebounder.

Personal example

This is what transpired for me, when my feeling nature
wanted conscious acknowledgment. I had suppressed and
repressed it for so long that I liken my experience to a
corked champagne bottle. The pressure within built up over
decades of not expressing my emotionality, to the point
where I was crying between sales calls. I rationalized, "Oh
it's just because I've been working too hard. What I need to
do is to schedule in some playtime." The "check-up from the
heart up" came when I actually was out doing a leisure
activity that I love to do, and even then I was crying. I had
for a long time been feeling what Mary Manin Morrissey, in
her book *Building Your Field of Dreams,* refers to as "divine discontent." I was living on automatic pilot and that which had
been satisfying and fulfilling had ceased to be so. The sad
part was that I ignored the subtle signals and pressed on. My
thoughts were, "Well, I've been through worse and I can get
through this." (This was a learned habit of abandonment of
self with respect to emotional availability.) When it was clear
that I wasn't coping and wasn't getting through this, I was
afraid because I thought I was going crazy, as I had never
been unable to control my emotions before.

In my despair, I went to see my doctor and requested
help. I made it clear that I did not want a prescription drug
medication. I wanted a professional referral so that I would
receive assistance from someone I could speak with. The
doctor gave me a phone number of the local mental healthcare team office. Plus, the prescription she did give me was
to take a minimum of four to six weeks off work.

The old paradigm and stigma attached to the idea of
reaching out beyond our family of origin stems from the

limiting belief of not airing your dirty laundry in public: "Keep quiet, don't tell anyone about your problems, be strong." Plus the limiting belief that only crazy people go to see psychiatrists. In my opinion, we do ourselves a great disservice when we do not speak our truth. Resources were not available to the earlier generations but they most certainly are now. There are so many service organizations that provide incredible assistance and support services within our communities now. The current trend is private coaching, if that is your personal preference. There is a wealth of information and options available. When we talk, share our stories and experience, we receive referrals, recommendations, and the help we so desperately need in order to create and thrive.

For decades, I had lived without allowing support in my life. Finally, I saw the value in having an impartial outside party as a great choice and starting point for me. It allowed me to get used to the idea that it's okay to ask for and receive help! It is not a sign of weakness to ask for assistance. It is a courageous choice for change. It's a huge wake-up call from the independence I had fought to realize for decades, to accept the truth of my interdependence. We need each other. You're on the earth to learn and grow through your relationships. Ann Mortifee in her song "Born to Live" said: "In every heart is an outstretched hand" – a statement that instigated a profound visual for me, of hands reaching from our hearts seeking for truth and for help along the way. I encourage you to just admit to yourself and say silently, "I need help. I desire help. I want help and I'm going to ask for help! I am going to invest time and energy in creating a system of support for myself."

I was finally ready to admit that a limiting belief I had

adopted with regard to my feeling nature no longer served me. I had shut myself down emotionally in order to stay safe and to be accepted, which gave birth to the macho aspect of me. What do I mean when I say "to stay safe?" In times of abuse, I learned it was better not to express myself, as it could have meant more violence. Then the flip-side of this same coin was that I not be needy either, because time and time again I had experienced how people were repulsed by my neediness and rejected me. Consequently, I learned to reject my own feelings and emotions. The choice and challenge is to effect a balanced, wholesome experience and that takes time, exploration, and practice. It is possible to accept the fact that emotions are energy, are part of the wholeness of my being, and that's okay.

Once I asked for help and actually spoke to a trained mental healthcare professional, the cork blew and the bubbles of my emotion spilled over the top. What a relief, the pressure was gone and for the first time I began to consciously acknowledge, and give myself permission to feel and express, my emotions.

What evolved from this process of learning to listen and to be available to myself was, and continues to be, a process of aligning my heart and mind systems of intelligence. It is invaluable to have each of them working together to advance each other, rather than one working to the exclusion of the other.

I told myself the truth. I was exhausted and did not want to push myself and achieve and do. The corporation that I was then working for was not a fit for me. I was forcing myself to work in a professional environment that conflicted with my personal values. Plus the most obvious truth was that my heart wasn't in it at all. This was one of the contributing factors to what I now call my "breakdown to break-through" season of my life.

If this resonates with you, take a moment to be with the waterfall, and this time focus on the rainbow. I've heard many times that the rainbow always appears after the rain or the storm. Rainbows have also been likened to hope. I would like to share a saying that I heard, because maybe it's time for you, as it was for me, "to give up all hope of a better yesterday." Know for yourself that hope is empowering in the moment you feel it and it can make a difference in your life, right here, right now – today!

Back to the personal example I was sharing. Through a referral from the mental healthcare professional, I heard about a career futures course and this supported me in discerning and choosing my next career. Then a series of experiential courses primed the pump for new avenues of self-study and exploration and questions: "Is this true for me? Is it something I adopted from someone else?" Quite a maturing process, despite already considering myself to be mature because of my age.

An integral part of learning to be available to myself in new ways was facilitated by my choosing to simplify my life. The career change I made at the time was one that provided me with more time to incorporate into my life all the intellectual knowledge I had learned and to now live it rather than read and learn about it. There was a huge difference between knowing something and experiencing it. In my case I chose to sell my home and free myself from a mortgage debt by getting something smaller. The hours of work shifted from outrageous to manageable. I made weekend retreats once a month rather than one big expensive holiday once a year. I stopped the human doing and began to experience myself as a human being. I spent a lot of time in nature, and through my nature experiences a process evolved which greatly assisted me.

The surprise for me was the departure from my normal nature activities to find myself compelled to simply be still. The acutely sensitive innate aspect of self awakened and I learned how to consciously attune to, and to perceive, subtle energy. My perceptive vision was enlivened. I am not speaking of my physical eyesight of the material world, but my perceptive vision with regard to the energetic world.

Exercise

Here is an easy five-step process I'd like to share with you. By the way, this process is not limited or reserved solely for you to use in nature. You can use it any time and any place that suits you. The five steps are:

> the quiet;
> the still;
> the fill;
> the knowing; and
> the movement.

You can use this exercise with regard to attuning to your body and its intricate system of energy. I will walk you through a process of locating an energy density within your physical self. Hopefully you will understand through experience what I mean by "unexpressed emotional energy creates an energy density within the physical body."

When you feel an achy pain in your body, lie on your

back on the floor or on your bed (or simply be still in a posture or position that is comfortable for you) and close your eyes to outer distractions. Relax, with your legs slightly apart and your hands with palms facing the ceiling about a foot away from your thighs. Focus your attention on your heart and take a few long, slow inhalations and exhalations as you attune to the energy of life, your breath, and your heartbeat (the quiet).

The next step is to breathe into the region of your body where you feel the stimulation, the signal, in order to decode the message (the still). This focuses your conscious attention on the part of your body giving you a message of pain, discomfort, tightness, itchiness, ache, etc. It is your way of being still to listen to your body, and you can even say aloud: "Okay body, you have my conscious attention, I listen now for you; tell me what it is you have to say." Then be patient with yourself and breathe into the spot slowly, with your full attention on this region of your physicality. You are innately capable of awakening your perceptive vision. You have the innate capability to perceive subtle energies.

The fill is the delivery of the message. Now there are limitless ways that the message may come forward to you. Here are a few examples.

> In the form of a flashback of a scene from the past.
> Emotions may run their course in the form of tears.
> You may smell something and then recall a memory.
> You may hear something.
> You may feel moved to touch, stroke, or massage

this part of your body.
You may move into a different position and
make sounds.

Your experience will be unique to you. With the fill, you receive your unique knowing (new understanding or awareness) and then, if necessary, the movement, which may be action or inaction.

In her book *Heal Your Body*, Louise L. Hay states, "Metaphysical causations describe the power in the words and thoughts that create experiences. An awareness to help us understand the connection between thoughts and the different parts of the body and physical problems."

Personal examples – body as messenger

In working with this technique, I have many examples I can share. One morning I was reluctant to go on my morning hike, which surprised me because I love to start my day in the forest and watch the sun rise. As I went up the mountain trail (the quiet), my legs became so heavy and sore that I could not continue. I had to stop and I sat down on the trunk of a fallen tree (the still). There I breathed into my legs and asked, "Tell me what it is, what is the message in this pain?" (the fill). Then came some scenes from the past (the knowing) and as I rubbed my legs (the movement), the tears flowed. The memory I recalled came forward to me, complete with strong smells and a taste in my mouth. In the use of this technique all senses are not necessarily involved in the process, but on this day that was what transpired. When I had finished being available to myself by allowing my body to deliver its message and by letting the emotion run its course, the pain eased and I became calm. I decided to go home because there was much for me to write in my journal. I gave myself the gift of time to feel, deal, and begin to heal that which was coming forward to me, in a way of ease by revealing my truth in the moment.

Sometimes in my experience the heaviness or pain moves upward through my body when dealing with a particular issue over a number of weeks or even a couple of months. On one occasion I had a muscle spasm in the lower region of my back, which put pressure on my sciatic nerve. I was in agony and spent time with myself to receive the messages from my body, in combination with chiropractic care and reflexology. During the next few weeks, I felt pain in the mid-back region of my body, opposite my heart. Then it proceeded to my entire left-wing region, including my heart, left breast, left clavicle, and my left shoulder. I experienced a sore, stiff neck for a couple days and then one morning my jaw locked when I yawned. It seemed that this was the path this energy needed to take in order for it to completely express itself and deliver the messages, and I could participate by doing the release work.

Ken Dychtwald, in his book *Bodymind*, explained this so well, and I understood what was transpiring during my intensely personal sacred healing journey: "As emotions flow upward from the belly and chest, they enter the neck where they are further translated from feelings into thoughts and words. Whereas the chest serves to expand and amplify these emotional flows, it is the neck's function to sort and refine them, dispatching them to their appropriate destination in the throat and face. The neck must continually mediate between feelings and thoughts, impulses and reactions. When the communication is more than the emotional and neuromuscular circuits can handle, the lines tend to overload and the Bodymind registers a signal, which is immediately felt as tension. By acting as a mediator between opposing forces, it tends to accumulate much of the stress of the conflict and can become annoyingly painful and tense. If some aspects of the conflict can be relieved, the neck becomes more able to relax and can then allow the healthy flow of energy upward and downward through the Bodymind."

Ken Dychtwald further states that "The oral segment – throat, chin, jaw – is responsible for a wide variety of expressive actions, such as talking, crying, laughing, biting, smiling, frowning, smelling, eating, spitting, screaming, and swallowing. Health and vitality in this region can be seen to correspond with the uninterrupted flow of such actions and emotions. On the other hand, when these actions are restricted from full animation, blockage and tension may result."

Example – body as messenger in relationship interaction

I was driving in the car with a soul friend en route to our destination, dinner, and a movie. I was asked to stop and do some errands. I felt a twinge of pain jump on the left side of my collarbone and this zinged up into my shoulder girdle. I was shocked by the intensity of the pain. I stopped as requested and opted to wait in the car. I knew I had at least half an hour, so I became quiet and still and breathed into the pain. What came up for me was a memory from the past, triggered by the present interaction with this soul friend. I felt manipulated. I had been invited to go to dinner and a movie and there was no mention of shopping or errands (a hidden agenda or expectation). I honored my feelings and allowed myself to vent my frustration and cry. I also said I would give myself more time and space when I got home. There were many past instances of manipulation that came forward to me in a way of ease for conscious acknowledgment and healing as a result of this one interaction.

The process of manipulation brought forward many examples for me to feel, deal, and heal. Plus, I had to reveal the truth to myself of all the past instances of when I was the manipulator. All the times in my relationship interactions when I had hidden agendas and unspoken expectations. Can you believe I even had expectations with regard to sentient beings, the dolphins when I went on a human-dolphin connection retreat? What you will realize is that as you wean yourself off the manipulation habit, you will probably not experience being manipulated. And you will recognize manipulation scenarios expeditiously and make appropriate decisions and choices to experience the results you desire based on your enhanced understanding and awareness.

Example - body as messenger in a self-study

An itchy rash developed across my pelvic girdle and mid-section. It was so irritating that I woke in the middle of the night, raking my body with my nails. I got out of bed and tried applying some healing balm to cool the area, but it didn't help. So annoyed and frustrated, I allowed myself to vent my anger. Then when I calmed down enough to be quiet I lay on the floor in the darkness. I breathed into the rash and said: "Okay rash, you have my attention, tell me what it is you have to say? What is itching to come out and express itself?" I was flooded by memories and spent much time allowing the emotionality to run its course.

After I was complete in that part of the process, I realized that many of the memories transpired in two specific locations that I saw repeatedly behind my closed eyes. The energy that I had taken on, which I had adopted from my interaction within these two institutions, was shame. For years I had carried energy that was not even mine. The obvious became apparent, and from my enhanced self-awareness I said, "I took on this shame and it wasn't even mine. I need to give it back. It is yours after all." As I spoke the words aloud, I imagined behind my closed eyes the shame energy flowing out from me and into the two institutions, and the people associated with the shaming. Throughout this visualization process, my abdominal and pelvic regions became very hot and then very cool, and I did not feel itchy any more. I flopped into bed and slept soundly. Over the next few days more incidents of shaming came forward for me to feel, deal, and heal by revealing the truth to myself. As I dealt with the issues the process evolved, I released the emotional energy, and wrote in my journal, and the rash gradually disappeared in a matter of days without a prescription. In this unique circumstance it was a non-medical issue.

This is a process to assist you in attuning to and decoding the messages of communication from your miraculous body. This holistic technique complements, and is to be used in combination with, your traditional healthcare practices, not to their exclusion. The main idea that Louise

L. Hays emphasizes in her books is to tell yourself the truth about your thoughts when it comes to your overall health and wellness. They may offer you some valuable clues and insights.

Exercise – separating from yourself energy that is not your own

Through self-study, when you become aware that you have adopted and taken on energy that does not belong to you, you can cleanse it from yourself. You can do an exercise I call the "return to sender" meditation to free yourself from the energetic enmeshment. You cleanse from your body the energy that you identify as other than your unique signature vibration, and send it back to the source. This is not to be done with malicious intent. This is simply your acknowledgment that you took something on that does not belong to you. You can cup the energy in your hands and, with a forceful exhalation, blow it into a violet flame, or you can imagine it to be surrounded with a white transformational light, or you can envision it returning to its source.

Get into a relaxed and comfortable position. You may choose to sit in a chair with your feet flat on the floor or lie down on your back on the floor. Take in a few deep cleansing breathes. Focus on the region of your body that you determine to be the location of the energy you adopted that is not your own. Meditation provides you with the ability to bend time in order to feel, deal, and heal any past event. You can imagine and replay the scene completely and when you get to the part when the words are spoken by the other person(s) involved, you pretend to wrap the words, action, energy of the circumstance in a bubble. This will separate the thought energy that you adopted from someone else and which is not your own. You envision the thought energy in any way you choose, with a unique size, shape, or color, and see it leaving your energy system, your body, and being returned to sender. Then imagine yourself being filled up with light and love from your own heart, and this expands until your entire body is in light.

Many times in your life, especially when you were young, you became emotionally and energetically enmeshed with those in your life. Up until now, you may not have known how to separate the energy of the words, actions, and thoughts of others from yourself. You took them to heart and literally stored this within your own system of energy. What a relief to learn and practice energy self-management and get acquainted with yourself as a system of energy. You have a unique signature vibration. What a gift to be able to cleanse and separate from yourself that which is not yours.

Example

Let's say as a child you were thirsty and did not want to bother your care-giver and you went to the fridge to get the big jug out and when you poured yourself a drink you spilled some of the liquid. Just then the care-giver comes into the room and yells and screams, calling you clumsy, and punishes you for making a mess. You are sent away, still thirsty. There is much that you may have taken on in this one scenario. You could have taken on the limiting judgment that you are clumsy. You could have taken on that you should not try to do things on your own because you make a mess and will be punished for attempting to make decisions and do things on your own. You may assume that you are not capable of attempting to do new things. You may believe that you are not worthy of satisfying your own thirst. Whatever your experience and response to this one event, it is unique to you and so is the process of feeling, dealing, healing, and revealing the truth of it to yourself. In any case, there may be energetic enmeshment that you now have the skill to separate from yourself.

Exercise – a self-assessment question

Here are some questions that will allow you to take more care with yourself as a system of energy. You can ask yourself: "What type of energy do I receive in this interaction? Is there any energy? If there is, what type is it? Do I feel it is supportive and beneficial to me or not? Do I wish to continue to receive this energy?" This way you can take more care with your unique signature vibration than you currently offer yourself. In your relationship interactions you know very clearly what you put forward at any given moment, and you know the truth of your intention. When you feel uncomfortable you can ask yourself the aforementioned questions.

What you learn through use of this type of self-assessment and observation exercise is that your thought and feeling energy have particular characteristics. As you practice energy perception you can identify the energy you put forward in your relationship interactions, which are a consequence of your thoughts and feelings. You learn to distinguish the characteristics of your own paranoia, anger, shyness, envy, fear, worry, anxiety, frustration, jealousy, joy, excitement, and so on, and this empowers you in your practice of energy perception and discernment. Then in your relationship interactions you are more able to perceive and understand the energy dynamics.

Personal examples of energy perception and discernment

There are always opportunities to practice energetic discernment and here are a few examples that will assist to explain this idea.

While conversing with an individual I sensed some uncomfortable energy as their partner walked toward us. In my silent check-in with myself I did not track the source of discomfort within me. I asked if in the moment my companion was feeling comfortable with the topic of conversation and he assured me that he was fine. When an opportunity presented itself for me to check-in with the partner, I inquired: "When you saw me standing and speaking with your friend I felt some uncomfortable energy and I was curious about it. I asked your partner if he was comfortable with the topic of conversation and he assured me he was okay. I'm curious to know if you were feeling particularly emotional when you approached the two of us earlier today? Is everything okay? Did it bother you that I was talking with him?" She said: "It didn't bother me.

However I did feel jealous." We walked and talked and she shared in depth how they had come to be traveling together. They were indeed just friends, and a couple days later, she came up to thank me for taking time to make the initial inquiry. She said that it assisted her to become clear enough as to her feelings towards her friend and her expectations of the relationship to be able to discuss them with him. I also thanked her for being willing to level with me, because it provided me with more trust in my instinct with regard to energy perception.

I entered an office boardroom and the energy was so dense that I literally bounced backward. There was an individual sitting at the table using a laptop computer. I asked him if he was okay. He said, "Yes, I'm fine, except I'm so frustrated with this – computer!" I inquired, "Is there anything in particular that I can help you with?" He replied, "No, I'll figure it out," and I promptly did what I had to do in the room and left him to his own devices.

I entered the home of a friend and immediately felt uncomfortable. I asked, "Is everything okay with you?" She responded, "No, you're early and I'm not ready and that makes me very angry, because I feel rushed!" "Oh," I responded "I'd be happy to leave and come back. How much more time would you like to have?" Plus, in the future, when I made plans with this individual I made a

point of never arriving early, to honor her clear
boundaries with respect to time.

Have you ever gone visiting and felt instantaneously uncomfortable once you step into the new environment? On the
surface everything appears to be okay, yet your energy
antennae are picking up a mixed signal? Have you ever had
a friend of the opposite sex that claims they are okay with
being just friends, yet you pick up mixed signals that make
you feel uncomfortable? Have you ever gone for a job interview and known from the feel of the place and the people
whether you would even enjoy working for the organization? Have you ever entered a social, spiritual, or business
gathering and had a feeling about it? Have you ever gone to
a shopping mall and come away feeling drained or
exhausted? Although energy perception is a natural ability,
these exercises and questions assist you to become more
conscious of, and attune to, your innate capability.

It is important in your practice of being more conscious
of energy that you check out your perception with others, so
that you do not make incorrect assumptions and misper-
ceptions. Another point to remember is that not everyone is
willing to honor their feelings, let alone tell you what is
going on for them in the moment. It is so important to
respect privacy. The best place to practice the technique is
with yourself first and as you gain confidence in your own
energy discernment then you can venture forth and
practice with others. The main purpose of working with this
valuable energy self-observation process is to become
familiar with your own signature vibration. To remember
your innate potential to perceive subtle energies within
yourself and in the sea of energy in which we live.

Imagination exercise

There is a daily energy exercise that you can do to support yourself before you begin your day. You can imagine that you are sitting or standing beneath a white stream of energy, as wide as is comfortable for you, and this white energy fills, purifies, and aligns the wholeness of your being. Then you can imagine another stream of red and gold energy coming from the centre of mother earth up through your feet and legs, and the wholeness of your being filling, grounding, and creating you anew in the moment. Then you can imagine that, as you breathe into your heart, the colored energy – red, gold, and white – mixes to become golden pink. Imagine this golden pink filling, balancing, and harmonizing the wholeness of your being. To complete the exercise, imagine a huge funnel above you, filled with silvery liquid similar to that on the surface of a mirror. When you are ready, imagine that this silvery liquid creates a mirror shield over the outside edge of your system of energy. You can even touch yourself in some way, to create a signal for yourself, or move your arms while you say silently to yourself, "Mirror shield on." This way, when you move about in your day, any energy that is not your own signature vibration bounces off, so to speak. When I feel particularly emotional and/or vulnerable at various times during my hike of my life adventure, I redo this exercise often throughout the day to support myself. It is making a conscious choice not to interact in the sea of energy we call our world. It is as though you put up a barrier and speak with others over the gate. At other times you can choose to be more energetically open and not feel as though you need the gate.

Facilitating energy expression through the use of sound

On one occasion while I was at home, excruciating pain in my lower back brought me to my knees. I moaned out loud and began to make the sound "oh, oh, oh." Intuitively I leaned forward to place my hands on the floor, and bending my arms I lowered myself to the floor and began to rock myself back and forth. The value in making sounds is that the vibration they carry can assist stagnant, stuck emotional energy within our bodies to move, to run its course. We can facilitate the expression of our own feeling nature, when there are no words. The ancient Hawaiians, in their Huna healing practices, used sound and speaking aloud, with various syllables as described by Enid Hoffman in her book *Huna – Beginner's Guide:* "Ma, Ha, He (hay), Hu (hoo), Na, Nu, and Ho." Instinctively you may sound a consonant, howl, whine, cough, sneeze, or experience dry heaves. These are some of the natural methods of expressing energy and allowing it to move. Many times I have experienced a combination of these natural methods and then amazingly the emotions begin to flow. The vibration of the sound stimulates the energy congestion or density and then the energy begins to flow.

During this self-facilitation process, a memory may be recalled. In my experience, when a memory is recalled it is because there is an energetic charge of suppressed emotion attached to the memory, which needs to be expressed. Your body is a miraculous messenger indeed and it continually communicates with you. All that is required of you is to learn the language of your body. One method you may choose to use is the five-step process, attuning to the subtle messages from your body, and learning through practice how to decode the messages that your body gives you. I do not advocate this process to the exclusion of professional, traditional, or holistic healthcare consultations. This is a skill-set, a tool to add to your self-care and healthcare practice, if it resonates true for you and if you benefit by practicing the technique. I know for myself that when I stopped medicating myself and taking prescription pain medication, I was able to receive and work through some of the unresolved emotional issues that I had stored within my physicality with regard to sexual abuse and acceptance of my femininity.

The idea of scanning your body can be used any time you feel the sensation of heaviness, pain, stiffness, muscle spasm, ache, or imbalance. Focus and pretend to breathe into the discomfort to activate your innate energy perception capability to discern:
what it was that created the density; and why and how it is to be released.

I have been known to read many books at the same time. Have you ever done that? Unfortunately, I read these words and wrote them down without noting their author. I give thanks for this information although I do not know to whom to give the credit. It may assist you in understanding the aforementioned idea of energy perception: "The body is affected by all thoughts. Brain consciousness becomes cell consciousness. Recovery is certain, an innate ability. The body is the servant of the mind. Cells say, 'If you change what you're sending us, we'll gladly cooperate if you will.' The body follows direction, circuited to the brain."

Personal example

One morning when I lay on my yoga mat to do some stretching, my upper arms were particularly sore and my left wing was very tight. I began to stroke and massage my upper arms and I could feel the lumps of congested energy beneath the surface of the skin. When I applied constant gentle pressure on one of the lumps, the energy began to run its course. Many memories came forward to me as I continued to apply gentle pressure upon my upper arms, then my left breast, left shoulder, the region between my shoulder and my neck on the left side. I experienced the sensation of heat from each region as the energy of the emotion released. Also the flesh would become red from the heat and the gentle pressure.

I wrote the detail in my journal about the many scenes of when I was bullied, hit, spanked, pinched, pulled, yanked, and the energy continued to flow. I realized that the people enacting the bullying and violence were not conscious of the effects of their acts. I remember on one occasion asking one individual, "Why do you hit me so much?" From the look on their face, they were not even conscious of the fact they had just hit me. I guess it was the face-to-face question that woke this person from their slumber and they never hit me again.

The consciousness of the energy of their anger, frustration, fear, grief of their thoughts, still exists. As a child I took it on. As a child, I was certainly not aware of how to separate the energy of someone else from my own energy, let alone distinguish it. For me there was the physical experience of each circumstance, the energy of their and my emotional energy in each particular event. The evolution of my process includes understanding my physical, energetic, emotional, psychological, and now physiological healing. This particular experience was my first with regard to acknowledging the consciousness of the thoughts I adopted from those enacting the bullying or the violence in addition to my own fear.

An "ah ha" moment for me with regard to this experience was a connection to what Jesus said in the Bible in Luke 23:34 – "Forgive them for they do not know what they do." Of course, people in their unskilled and acting-out behavior were not conscious of the severe consequences of their actions. I had been bitter and resentful for nearly three decades because of the brutality and violence I experienced in my youth, from sources too many to mention, and now with divine assistance I can work toward freeing myself from my own condemnation.

Bullying is frequently in the news and the devastating consequence of youth and teen suicide is a wake-up call for all of us. There is power in the consciousness of the energy of each thought, word, and deed. What is your intent? Is it a thought, word, or deed that is life-giving or is it something else? You are response-able to choose and ask yourself, "Is it for the highest good of all?" Remember to consider the consequences of the energy of your thought, word, or deed. Is it life-giving, positive, and uplifting or is it destructive, depressing, and negative?

Learning about the energetic emotional component of myself helped me to understand and identify how I gained so much weight during particularly emotionally charged seasons of my life. Like when I worked in a volatile workplace and gained fifty pounds. I ate and stored my anger, chewing my words rather than expressing them another way. The energy of my thoughts has an impact on my body and on those about me. When I was healing the impact of the sexual and physical abuse issues, my inner child compelled me to put on an armor of protection. I felt small, unsafe, and scared. To support myself I would affirm often: "I am safe, I am secure."

Another experience was when I got an itchy rash on the inside of my thighs. I would wake in the middle of the night, raking my thighs with my nails, from the heat and the frustration at not being able to ease the itchiness. I would get out of bed, lie on my yoga mat, do the five-step process, and say: "Okay, what is itching to come out and be acknowledged by me? I listen now for you. What is this all about?" I could not believe the process that evolved – many days of dreams with various people coming forward to me reminding me of my past.

It was through this process that I finally acknowledged a whole heap of guilt energy that I had been carrying for years. I had been celibate by choice for a season of my life, as I still carried guilt for my years of acting-out behavior of sexual promiscuity decades earlier. The events played across the projector of my mind and as I cried and released this guilt energy, the heat that came off my legs was amazing. When I was complete, after each session I would imagine with each breath that the light from within my heart expanded to fill my entire body with soothing golden-pink energy. This is the color I use to symbolically represent unconditional love. If, while a scene replayed, I realized that I had adopted the guilt energy from something someone else had said to me, through the use of my vivid imagination I would simply send the energy back to them or blow it into an imaginary violet flame for transformation. In due time, after many pages of journal writing, work with my therapist, energy work with a holistic healer, emotional release work, art therapy, saltwater baths, the rash disappeared.

Exercise

Each time you are quiet and still and tune into the physical pain, soreness, ache, stiffness of your body, be available to yourself and you will receive wonder. Your body is miraculous. I encourage you to ask for divine assistance by saying, "I willingly surrender and release _____ [fill in the blank with the specific energy you have identified that you wish to release]. I open to receive divine light and love and to fill this region of my body with vibrant new consciousness." In addition you can affirm some truths if this idea resonates with you. Some simple affirmations I use are: "I am safe, I am secure." And a great resource book for affirmations is *Meta Fitness - Your Thoughts Taking Shape: You Can Change Your Body With The Power of Your Mind,* by Suzy Prudden and Joan MeijerHirschland.

Facilitating energy expression through creativity

Creative expression can be a window into self. Criticisms and grades from the past may have had a debilitating effect on your creative desires. They may have even completely blocked access to your innate capability to express yourself creatively. Before you attempt a creative expression session, have a dialogue with your inner critic. You can say whatever comes to you, but here is an example: "Inner critic, I'm asking you to take a break, a back seat, and allow for the expression of my creative self. I am not casting you aside and you are not going to die. I do appreciate all you have done, all the ways you protected the child I once was from getting hurt. I am perfectly safe at this time and have no need for your protection. Right now, I need to explore my creative self and provide a new opportunity for expression. Thank you, inner critic, I do appreciate you, enjoy your rest."

Why is it so important to make time for such a dialogue with yourself? The dialogue is giving permission to surrender control and is allowing your creative energy to express itself without restrictions or limitations. It is not appropriate for you to sit down and allow the intellect to plan what it is you are going to create. You do need to know the medium you desire to work with, so you can prepare or purchase the supplies. For instance, if you wish to paint, color, sculpt with clay, or do a collage, you need the items in front of you in order to do the exercise.

Creativity exercise

Once you have your supplies in front of you, sit down and relax. Have a silent or out-loud verbal dialogue with your inner critic, using either the sample dialogue I suggested or your own. Then close your eyes and give invitation to your creative self in thoughts that flow naturally and feel comfortable. Then be quiet and be still and focus your attention on your breath. Totally relax, just be in the moment and do not move until the energy of the creativity moves through you. Remain in the silence and enjoy the process. This could take a few minutes or it could take an hour. Your process will be unique to you.

Personal example

During a one-week intensive, I was guided through this exercise, and for my art medium I chose clay because I remember having so much fun with it when I was very little. In a brief meditation, I had a silent dialogue with my inner critic and gave invitation to my creative self. I closed my eyes and waited, focusing on my breath with my hands on the table touching a lump of clay. When I felt compelled to take action I began squishing the clay between my fingers, working it, warming it, and making it more flexible. I molded a totem-like structure. The torso of a feminine body form on one side, and a serpent body with an owl's face on the other. When I felt as though it was complete, the practical part of me decided that the totem would be useful as a candleholder. I made an impression in the top with my thumb, wide and deep enough to hold a candle. When I turned to enjoy this creation I noticed that from the last gesture, the eyes of the owl were now closed.

The sculpture was a creation with a message from an aspect of myself that rarely had the chance to express itself. I pondered the significance and symbolism of the headless female torso. It dawned on me that the torso houses the heart. I have spent the majority of my adult life in my head, in my intellect, and expressing my masculine active/doing nature. My attention was being called to allow my heart, my feelings, my emotions, and my feminine receptive nature to be awakened and acknowledged as part of the wholeness of my being. I was curious about the significance of the serpent with the face of an owl. What are the characteristics represented by these two animals? When I fashioned the finished piece into a candleholder, the eyes of the owl closed. Clearly, this spoke to my heart and said: "I do not acknowledge my own wisdom, my instincts, my intuition, and my innate clairvoyant capabilities." The snake was upright and rising like a cobra. A cobra is a very powerful snake and has sensitivity to vibration frequencies of energy. This window through the image of an animal gave me an opportunity to pay more attention to what most resonates with me. What feels right for me and what does not. Incidentally, I have never liked snakes throughout my life so it was so surprising to me that I sculpted one. There was much more that came to me when I looked at this totem over the next few months. I did do a number of pieces and each was a unique and valuable window into myself.

Exercise – collage creativity

To make a collage you require a piece of poster cardboard, which can be any color, a number of old magazines, a glue stick, a pair of scissors, and some felt pens. The dialogue with your inner critic is important. The request for your creative self is slightly different. One intention of making a collage is as a goal-setting mechanism guided by your soul rather than your personality. You ask for assistance and support through this creative medium, for support with a particular issue, or to create a visual one-month, six-month, one-year, or even a five-year goal plan, through the use of pictures and words gathered from magazines. You ask for a balanced, wholesome approach to goal-setting, with consideration given to each of the four quadrants of life: health, wealth, career, and relationships. Health incorporates the physical (recreation, and mental, emotional, and spiritual wellness), and wealth includes abundance in all aspects of life, not just with respect to money.

Do the exercise in silence and do not move until the energy moves you. You will be amazed at how quickly you collect specific photos and words. Intuitively you'll organize what you've gathered, cut, and paste, and in no time at all your collage will be complete. You sit back and review the entire thing as if you were explaining it to someone else. Feel the feelings of satisfaction and excitement as you visually go through your collage. Write in your journal your initial impressions, insights, and interpretation of what you have just created. The best place to hang this is where you can see it first thing in the morning and last thing at night. Each time you look at it, really tune into your feelings as you imagine whatever it is as real. I have had so much success using collages over the past fifteen years or so. Personally, I make one every five years, and most of what appears on the collage I actually experience in the five-year time-frame following completion of the creativity exercise. I know you will enjoy the process. You are free to be flexible to make the exercise workable for yourself.

Nature and your innate ability to perceive energy

I am sure you've got the idea of how you can attune to your body as a miraculous messenger. The five-step process is very versatile and I know that you will enjoy working with this technique. Another way you can use this technique is to heighten and expand your perceptive vision by doing open-eye meditations in nature. By being still and quiet, Spirit expressing through nature can assist you. The fill and the knowing come through your heart's ability to perceive the essence of the energy of life in a myriad of forms. An open-eye meditation is a way of attuning to the energy around you that supports you. Assistance is available from Spirit at all times – an ever-present help without limitation, unless you place a limitation upon it. In order to perceive the assistance and support, you need to be open and receptive, with your attention focused on the present moment.

The most expeditious way to bring your attention into the present while in nature is to give thanks for your present moment environment. Give thanks and be grateful for your physical senses. Your grateful heart is an open heart and your open heart has the innate capability to perceive subtle energy.

Personal example

What am I in nature? What do I identify with? I was asked this question during a week-long intensive workshop. I was asked to go outdoors in silence for an hour and, when we reconvened, to share a few sentences about the experience. This is my journal entry with the detail of my first open-eyed meditation experience in nature.

"I identify with the ocean, always moving. Sometimes I cover up my feelings like the water over the sand. Other times I retreat, search within myself, open up, identify, become aware, curious, like when the tide goes out. Sometimes I accept encouragement from others, accept nurturing, accept approval, and accept surprises, like the ocean when it receives raindrops or snowflakes. Sometimes I cry, release, like the bubbles from a gentle wave after it has broken against the shore. I experience storms in my life and allow the circumstances to beat me up like crashing waves. Other times I harness the energy and throw myself into a goal. I feel serenity after the storm. I calmly accept life's lessons and I am encouraged, hopeful, ready to keep going and growing. Sometimes I glow and sparkle and twinkle when the sun or moon are reflected upon me. I influence lives positively and negatively depending on the light I mirror.

"I am warm and cold depending on the atmosphere, the events that touch my life daily. I sometimes swirl with confusion like the riptides, which always open me up for self-discovery. I influence numerous individuals in my life as I am influenced by all living creatures in my world. I cannot be independent as I live and commune with others and share resources. I am aggressive and I am soft as I move through life.

"I am a vehicle, others learn from my experiences when opportunities present themselves, and we share openly, honestly. I bridge the gap between lands. I have friends all over the world; ties in different lands. I am touched by an incredible number of people. I am life-giving when I share myself with others. Others are nurtured and I am fulfilled. I have incredible dimension, insight, positive and negative qualities, like the ocean that holds living and dying things. I have hidden treasures to be discovered as I go. I have incredible adventure ahead of me. I touch many shores, I have unlimited potential and untapped resources. I reflect back to others what they see in me."

Incidentally, years later, when I was studying hatha yoga and living in an ashram in India, my yoga Swami presented me with the name "Shaygar," which means the ocean.

Have fun as you practice awakening your innate capability to perceive the unique energetic expression of Spirit expressing in and through life in a myriad of forms. All it takes is an open, receptive heart.

Exercise – open-eye meditation

I invite you to do an open-eye meditation. First, relax and be comfortable. Follow the five-step process as a guideline. Be still, be quiet, ask for the fill, receive the knowing, and then take action or inaction, the movement. The question I encourage you to ask yourself (the request for the fill), if you choose to do an open-eye meditation, is: "What am I in nature? What do I identify with?"

Open-eye meditation is just one of the myriad methods of meditation that you can use to assist and support yourself. You are free to explore and discern for yourself with which methods you are most compatible. After all, only you know what resonates with you and only you know what is best for you at any given moment. Meditation can assist you to transform knowledge of your physical, intellectual, energetic, and emotional aspects into understanding. Meditation can assist you so that each step you take in life, you take from a base of trust and a place of inner stability. Give yourself permission to use what works for you and create your own repertoire of meditation practices rather than attempt to fit yourself into a constrictive box created by someone else.

Personal examples
Size determines not your gracefulness and beauty

When I arrived in Hawaii near the end of my two-year world pilgrimage, I needed to purchase a bathing suit. I can tell you it was not a rewarding experience. I couldn't find anything that suited me. I gave up, feeling really depressed. My destructive self-talk was having a heyday in my head. My inner critic was brutal. I was upset and became tearful, so I got off the bus at an isolated lava-rock beach. I allowed myself to cry and was emotionally available to myself and let the frustration energy run its course. When I felt complete, I was calm and quiet and sat staring out over the ocean waves. I was grateful for the light dancing as it sparkled on the surface of the water. I could feel the mist against my cheeks and taste the salt on my lips. I could smell the sea, and I became mesmerized by the rhythm of the waves breaking against the rocks.

All of a sudden a whale jumped up right in front of me, in breach position. I was startled and awestruck in the same moment. My jaw dropped and, with my mouth hanging open, I stared wide-eyed at the whale. This spectacular mammal seemed to be suspended in the air. In slow motion the glistening water ran off its mammoth body and fins. Then the whale disappeared into the ocean depths through the middle of its own re-entry splash. My mouth was still hanging open when it jumped again and my grateful open heart perceived this message: "Your size does not determine your gracefulness and beauty. Look at me, I weigh many tons, I have no waistline yet you are in awe and stunned by my beauty and magnificence. Beauty is not made of shape and form, it shines from within like a star. Your beauty is within you and it is limitless. Size determines not your gracefulness and beauty. Embrace yourself and say 'I love you truly'."

I invite you to take a few moments and do this affirmation exercise. First fill in the blank with your name and affirm: "_____, size determines not my gracefulness and beauty. I embrace myself and say that I love myself truly. I am full of grace and beauty."

Kind acts and wisdom of ants

While living at an ashram in Rishikesh, India, it was necessary for me to make some adjustments in order to adapt to the environment and the customs. One such adjustment was at mealtimes. In the dining hall we sat on the floor and also used the floor as a table. Consequently, we shared our table (the floor) with other creatures, including a family of ants. By keeping a watchful eye on my plate upon the floor, I was able to make sure I did not get any unexpected protein with my vegetarian meals. I have to admit that I found the ants to be really annoying at mealtimes. I was so frustrated that I stayed away from the dining hall for a few days.

One morning, to my shock and initial dismay, the ant family visited my room. Overnight I had inadvertently left a metal cup half full of soda on the end table next to my bed. What follows is what I perceived and wrote in my journal.

> "There were many ants having a sip, one was even taking a dip. Each one that found the cup climbed up and over the top. Down inside and back out again, their duty did not stop. They took extra on each antenna and with another they did share. It made my heart dance to see how for each other they did care. Still others roamed blindly, not aware of the feed. An ant aware of the source would take the lead. Two-by-two they came up the leg of the table. Climb this metal cup, it is no fable. Amazing to see how the ant family distributed the food. Everyone had some for the highest good. I thought this little insect was a six-legged pest. Wow, did my perception get put to the test. They instinctively walk each other home, leaving not one alone to roam. They cohabit and share any society, with no one expecting notoriety. The size, the color, or the strength of the ant mattered not. These innocent creatures knew not what they taught. Thank you ants for being so smart. Teaching me how to open my heart. You demonstrated distribution and equality. I'll share the concept with humanity."

There really is no limit on what, where, when, how, or from whom we can learn, unless we limit ourselves.

Everything is energy

If you are willing to entertain the notion that everything is energy, with its own unique signature vibration, you will find this example most interesting. I would like to speak with you about books, photographs, and places. Is it possible that you and I are eternal infinite expressions of Spirit, and as such Spirit remembers all of the vibrations of experience through which it passes, even if one is not conscious of the fact? Many times I have been asked the question, "How did you plan your world pilgrimage?" The answer, herewith, demonstrates that it was not a plan as much as a guiding through a series of circumstances.

I started with a landscape photography book called *The Sacred Earth* by Courtney Milne. I felt drawn to it at a bookstore, picked it up and was really in awe of it. The logical, rational part of me said, "It's just after Christmas, it's too expensive, put it back." I listened to my logic, put the book down, and left the store. That evening I woke up from my sleep when I heard, "Go buy the book." Groggy, I simply rolled over and went back to sleep. A short time later I again woke up to the message, "Go buy the book," and again I chose to roll over and go back to sleep. The third time, the message was so loud that I sat bolt upright in bed and said aloud: "Okay, okay, I got the message, now can I please get some sleep?" The following morning when I woke up, I felt frantic inside and was compelled to call the store and ask that the book be put aside so that I could come during my lunch hour to pick it up. When I went to pay the cashier, she asked a fraction of the cost written on the price tag. I did not realize that the store was having its annual end-of-year inventory reduction sale.

On the weekend I lay down on the floor to read this book. An entire day passed and I did not budge until I was finished. The best way I can describe what happened in my interaction with this book was that at certain times I felt such a strong resonance with certain photographs that it felt as though I went right into the picture. I did not understand this intense unfamiliar connection, yet it was incredibly significant.

A year later, while on a guided nature excursion on the island of Kauai, one of the Hawaiian Islands, something very profound happened. We had been asked to come on our own to a particular beach and meet at a certain time. When my feet touched the beach, I felt this frantic feeling within me while I had the thought, "I have to find a rock! I have to find a rock!" I don't know if you've ever been on a Hawaiian beach, but they are made up mostly of huge black lava-rocks and sand that has been brought to the islands. I was attracted to a trail on the perimeter of the beach and as I walked along it I looked for a rock. I noticed I was getting a distance away from the group gathering together on the beach and since I did not know where we were going I became a bit nervous. I kept going and soon I found and picked up a rock. It was dirty beige in color and rather large. Immediately the frantic feeling stopped and I quickly made my way to the group of folks gathering on the beach. My car was close so I put the rock in the trunk of the car, thinking: "I don't know how I'm gonna pack that to go home, it's so large – oh, well!"

I joined the circle and we stood while our facilitator explained the nature excursion exercise. We were going to an ancient temple ruin site. It is a very powerful place, so we must be clear with our intentions. In order to honor each other's process, we were to proceed in a line, single file, barefoot if we wished, and in silence. Then the facilitator said that when they visited the sacred site the ancients would always bring a love offering, "a rock wrapped in a leaf." My knees buckled from under me and I would have fallen down had I not been holding hands with the others. When our circle broke up I retrieved the rock from the car and picked up a leaf from the ground on the trail as we proceeded. Incidentally, the trail we were on was the exact trail on which I had found the rock.

I made my way up the trail to the top of the hill. I felt as though there was a magnet inside that automatically pulled me toward a huge rockface. When I left the trail I ascended a set of stairs to find an altar carved into the rock wall. With both feet on the top step I closed my eyes and silently gave thanks and began to pray my silent intentions. The rock I was holding grew hotter and hotter until I had to put it down on the altar, and my hands slapped together in prayer position at my heart centre. The closest description I can give you to describe being held in this intense energy vortex, as numerous waves of energy washed over me, is being under a waterfall.

When the energy stopped flowing, I went down the steps to the grass and just sat there, not understanding what had just happened. I wanted to ground myself and be still. I had barely recovered from the event when I was guided to walk over to the edge of the cliff. When I looked down to the ocean below, I saw a huge wall of water as two waves collided. I silently exclaimed: "This is where Courtney Milne took his picture!" I got my confirmation of a truth for me, the Holy Spirit Rush, and the fine hair on my body stood up and I had gooseflesh that was so strong that I had to sit down again. I couldn't wait to get home, to look at Milne's books. *Spirit of the Land* had been published as well. This time when I went through the books, I paid close attention to the resonance with each particular photograph, and created a list. It was this list of places that made up the destinations to which I journeyed during my two-year worldwide pilgrimage. What evolved was an incredible journey with Spirit, a walk of faith. I knew the name of the countries and some of the sights and ancient cultures that were calling me to experience, but I had no detail of what would transpire, and where I would stay.

Back to our story of the ancient temple ruin. I thought it important to point out that one of the most intriguing photos from *The Sacred Earth* book when I initially looked at it was called "Fan wave." I read how Milne had carefully descended the cliff upon which I had stood to take the fan wave photo from the beach below the temple ruin site.

Two years after this experience I returned to the island of Kauai, and learned that the ancient temple ruin I had visited was called a Heiau. The art of hula was taught there. This explained what happened the day after my initial visit to the sacred ancient temple ruin site two years earlier. Rather than stay in the bed and breakfast place, I asked some soul friends if I could stay on the beach with them, three hundred steps below our accommodation. They graciously agreed and offered me one of their tents. Around the campfire that night we were drumming and singing under the starlit sky. My feet were moving, keeping rhythm with the music, and one of my companions said to me: "Lorill, your body wants to move, get up and dance." I replied, "By myself?" They encouraged me: "Don't be shy, just dance."

As it happened, the night before, we had been given a hula demonstration. The gifted artist explained that the ancients used to use dance and song to pass on the wisdom of the ages, as they had no official language. The idea of hula is to be barefoot and first be quiet, be still, and do not move until the energy moves you. Does this sound familiar? Remember the five-step process we discussed earlier?

Choosing to listen to my body, I dutifully got up and stood barefoot in the sand by the campfire, with my eyes closed, and I did not move until the energy moved me. I danced for a long time, which felt like a few minutes. At the end when I stopped, I threw my arms above my head in a V for victory shape, at which time lightning streaked across the night sky. Excited, I ran to my friends around the campfire and asked, "Did you see the lightning? Did you see the lightning?" They said, "No." They asked if I had my journal with me and left me with the invitation to write down everything I remembered about the dance. Sitting inside my tent with a flashlight held against my chest with my chin, I began to write. As I wrote, I began to weep, when I realized I had just danced my life for these soul friends.

My intention in sharing these stories with you is this – although we are attracted through the resonance of the energy of people, places, and things, the logical, rational mind may object. Listen to the wisdom of your heart. When you allow your heart and brain systems of intelligence to work together to advance each other, rather than one working to the exclusion of the other, you will receive and experience wonder.

Exercise

If you scan your life, you will come up with examples of how you were drawn to speak to a particular person, drive a certain route, purchase a book, or attend an event, not fully understanding the compulsion to do so, yet you knew, you just knew that you had to. This is what I've been talking about.

Here is an idea that will assist you in learning the language of the heart. When you receive an impulse and you are uncertain and you wish to provide yourself with more clarity as your heart speaks truth to you, do not process through the intellect to come to logical, rational understanding, speak to the heart instead. Say, "Okay heart, I don't understand what you're saying. I understand that the heart is communicating. I am having difficulty decoding the message. Kindly give it to me in another way, a way that is more compatible with me, and in the most gentle way possible."

Do this so that you are not unclear with the messages your heart gives to you in the way that it does. You can develop a rapport relationship with your heart, so that you can request attunements and realignments. You can even say, "Look, this is great, but how about if we get something more subtle or a little stronger, or a little more clear, because I really do want to listen."

Dreams and your sleep-time provide incredible insight

I invite you to think of your sleep-time as a very valuable learning time. Whenever you have an issue that you're working on or through and you wish to have some divine support, you can request help before turning in for the night.

"God [or higher self, Holy Spirit, or however you wish to address the God of your understanding with your request for help], I dedicate my sleep-time to you. Teach me what I most need to learn at this point of my spiritual evolution. Let it be in a way that is most compatible with me, in a way of ease, and in the most gentle way possible. I ask for conscious memory of the lesson, dream, or symbol upon waking so I may journalize and ponder the teaching for the highest good of all. Thank you. Amen."

Also, when an issue wishes to make a transition from your unconscious into your conscious mind, one of the most gentle compatible ways is for the issue to make itself known to you in your dream process. Endeavor to note significant dreams in a journal on waking, and ponder the significance.

Personal example

Once when I used this technique I had a dream about a female friend. In the dream this dear one died. I was in distress about this dream. However, when I attended a workshop a few days later, one of the facilitators spoke on the subject of dream interpretation. (This reminded me of the familiar cliché: "when the student is ready the teacher appears.") He asked for examples from the participants and I volunteered to share my dream. When I was complete in describing the details of the dream he asked me, "What do you have in common with this person?" My immediate response was, "She does not do emotions." This was by her own admission, by the way. When a conversation became sentimental, her reaction was: "Can't go there, remember I do not do emotions." The facilitator then suggested that I ponder the fact that perhaps this part of me that related to that part of her is what is dying. My habitual behavior of not doing my emotions was coming forward because it no longer served me. In the dream she dies, when in fact it is the part of me that does not do emotions that is dying.

Further explanation

Many times when I worked with this technique, requesting that my sleep-time be used as valuable teaching time, I would wake up with the lyric of a song on my mind. This line became my positive mantra to provide support in order to deal effectively with my issue or support myself during that day. Spirit will communicate with you in the way that is most compatible with you. I love music and very often I receive encouragement and support from lyrics from a song playing on the radio, a song from a movie, a familiar lyric from a familiar song from my past, or a whole new song births itself through me.

One time during my commute to work I was thinking how I really did not enjoy the company of some of my co-workers. A familiar saying came forward to me in a lyric, complete with a melody, that bubbled up from within me when I stopped thinking and was quiet as I continued my journey to work: "Namaste, a simple word to say, feel its meaning within your heart today!" What a wake-up call from Spirit to acknowledge the light and love within each workmate and not focus on the unskilled, acting-out behavior which I took exception to. It certainly made a difference in my day.

Another time I had been on the receiving end of some fear-filled judgments with regard to selling my material possessions to make my world pilgrimage. I was crying as I drove myself home and my mind raced with thoughts of doubt. "Maybe they are right, maybe I am crazy like they say." In my doubt and confusion I prayed: "God, what am I to do? Am I to go or stay? Are they right? Have I made a mistake in my discernment and my choices?" I cried for a while longer and then became quiet. Then I felt a sudden impulse to turn on the radio in the car. So I did and I heard: "Hold onto your dream. Though no one else may see or understand, hold onto your dream." There was also more in the song that touched my heart and massaged my soul. I could hardly believe my ears. When I got home I called the radio station and found out the name of the artist and the title of the song. I went to the local store to purchase the music and when the clerk told me which CD the song was on, I laughed right out loud. You see, I had won that CD and picked it up from the radio station earlier in the week, and I had not had the time to listen to it yet.

Many times I would have a dream that involved an animal. Then I would look up the animal in a tremendous resource book by Ted Andrews entitled *Animal Speaks*, to read and ponder what message the animal may be bringing to me. This book is a significant resource in assisting me to understand the symbolism and characteristics of totem animals. Many ancient cultures have considered animals as teachers. Remember that there are limitless opportunities for us to learn and grow with Spirit expressing through a myriad of forms.

It is difficult to describe in detail the benefit of using this technique because each of us is on our intensely unique and personal hike of our life adventure. The main point I wish to make is that there is always support from Spirit available to us in a myriad of forms and our experience will indeed be unique. We attune to our innate capability of accepting and receiving this limitless support in the manner that is most compatible. I cannot tell you which methods will work best for you. All I can do is encourage you to be open to practicing various techniques and you will reap the rewards. Only you know what resonates true for you.

Go ahead and prepare the way

As a young child I was dragged off my bicycle and bitten by a dog, and for many years I was afraid of dogs. Even today, if a large dog approaches me excitedly I contract and tense up. What I know about myself is that when I am really afraid I seem to hold my breath. When watching movies with friends and the action in the film is rather intense, they say, "Breathe Lorill, breathe!" For me this is a wonderful support, because the last thing I want to do is to store tension and fear in my body. When I breathe I keep the energy moving. I have also had others tell me to breathe when I have been choked up with emotion. The reminder to breathe assists me to relax and honor my feelings and emotions. Speaking of honoring feelings and emotions, if you are ever present when an adult starts to cry, simply place a box of tissues near them and honor their emotions by allowing them to express themselves. Unless they request you to hold them or touch them, do not do so. In my experience, when someone touches me or consoles me it disrupts the natural flow of the emotional energy. Honor the individual and allow them to experience their emotional release until it has run its course. It is an incredible gift to be present and be a silent witness as a means of support.

During one of my house/dog-sitting experiences, I had the pleasure of walking two wonderful dogs twice a day. On one of our typical afternoon ventures we were challenged by five barking dogs. I did not have leashes with me because the dogs were so well trained and behaved. My heart pounded in my chest as we raced down a trail away from the main road. When we were safely away from the five barking dogs, I was hit with a wave of emotion. I know it was from the past and had been triggered by this current event. My companion dogs were so gracious and intuitive. They just lay down at my feet, while I allowed my emotions to run their course. When I was complete, I sat and rested for a short time and then my fear came up again because that was the only route back to the homestead and how were we going to get past those five dogs.

Now let me share what happened on the return journey to the homestead. Sure enough, when we got back up onto the main road, the dogs were there to greet us once again, barking, and moving in our direction. I commanded my two dog companions to stay and sit, and they dutifully obeyed. I breathed a few long, slow inhalations and exhalations into my heart centre and envisioned a huge beam of light and love energy emanating from my heart going to the other dogs and surrounding them. Standing still, silently in my mind and in the direction of the five barking dogs I formed these words: "You are safe and we will not harm you. We will be about our business and make our way home. We need to pass you. We desire the distance between us to remain the same. We ask that you do not come any closer to us than you are right now."

I stood still, continuing to visualize the light and love energy in their direction. The fear came up for me a little as the dogs and I made a step in their direction, so I commanded my companions to stay and sit one more time. I stayed still until I was calm once again and redid the exercise. When I took the initial step the second time, I focused on being in the light and love stream of energy. What amazed me was that the dogs backed up with each step I took in their direction and this time they were the ones to leave the main road, backing up all the while. The distance between us remained constant, although they continued to bark. We passed and made it to the homestead without incident.

Exercise example

Our thoughts are powerful energy, and visualization, meditation, and imagination exercises are very versatile. The example above is simply an exercise that you can do any time that you are worried, fearful, or anxious about an event. Be still, be quiet, focus on your heart centre, breathe deeply, and imagine your innerlight going ahead of you to prepare the way. Remember the poem/song at the beginning of the book? Your heart is your divine connection to spirit. Well, this is a consciousness-raising exercise. It is requesting divine assistance and co-creating in partnership. You can call upon the God of your understanding and request that it go ahead and prepare way. This could be a daily practice, even to light the way for a safe commute to life-giving appointments, by beaming love to all those you know you'll interact with in your day, filling your office, your home, and your car or whatever else you desire. It's a visual way of affirming the silent intention: "Inner light/love, go ahead and prepare the way for _____ [fill in the blank with your clear, conscious intention]." To ensure I am clear in my intent and do not use this technique in a self-serving manipulative manner, I personally like to add "… for the highest good of all." Be creative and enjoy working with this technique. You can use it before:

> booking a business appointment or applying for a job;
> selling a home, business, or vehicle;
> making contact for reconciliation with a dear one;
> traveling by plane, boat, car, bus, rapid transit;
> studying for exams and writing tests;
> doing volunteer service; or
> saying a final goodbye to a soul before they make their transition.

I worked with this technique very frequently when I was traveling with myself around the world. Each time I sat in a vehicle of any description, I would envision the white light and love energy around the entire vehicle. I would also fill the vehicle with it and ask for safe passage from point A to point B. There are limitless possibilities of using this technique or variations of it, so be conscious in your practice and enjoy your experience.

Exercise – a grateful way to close each day

A life-giving practice for the end of each day is with thanks-giving to the God of your understanding for the gift of life, for new understandings, growth, challenges, and blessings. You may also elect to include a request for a blessing to all the dearly departed souls that you have known in this lifetime and who have made their transition from life on earth to life after life. You may wish to give thanks for all your life experiences up until now. Perhaps give thanks for the past and God's mercy, the present and God's grace, and the future and God's providence. All we have are our expe-riences. It is not a matter of what happened but rather of whom we become as a result of moving and growing through our experiences. Then, of course, you can give thanks to God for those people who are in your life now. Give thanks for all with whom you have interacted as you learn to develop life-giving, loving, respect-filled relationships.

I invite you to relax with this poem before you leave the waterfall vista.

Peace is Possible – One Heart At a Time

I've got a dream, a dream of world peace.
I know that peace begins within me.
There is a spark burning deep in my core,
Yearning to be freed from captivity.
I release the pain, the pain of my past.
The past no longer binds my energy.
Now I know, I am connected,

Heart, body, mind, and soul.
I honor, love, accept, all that I am.
I was blind, now I see, I am open, I am free.
Now I see all of you in me.
I trust, surrender all, let my soul lead the way.
Yes, I can love eternally.
I've got a dream, a dream of world peace.
Come dream this dream of peace with me.
Peace in reality begins with me.

It is time to turn away from the waterfall and rainbow vista and continue on your way. I invite you to walk toward the magnificent forest. There are thousands of trees beckoning to you to come and be nurtured beneath their branches and limbs. In the silence, surrounded by an incredible variety of trees, your heart is stirred and you perceive this message from Spirit expressing in and through nature.

"How does a tree begin? A tree begins from a simple seed. A seed planted and nourished by the refreshing rain and caressed by the wind. A seed daily woken with the morning dew then warmed, hugged, and loved by the sun. A seed blanketed with the snow in winter or the moss during the rainy season. This seed regenerates and sleeps under the twinkling stars and the brilliant multidimensional moon. A simple seed, a mysterious creation. A seed so small and yet it bursts forth and grows, and over time manifests into a tree. A unique creation, one of the numerous varieties of trees we see upon the earth. A distinguishing realization is that there are no two trees that are identical. Many trees, many different shapes, and many different sizes, yet every tree we have ever seen began the same, with a simple seed.

"Each tree is free to be a tree. At one, in the moment, individual yet a part of the whole forest. Look, the tree boughs are touching and interwoven. What is the commonality of humanity? The commonality of humanity is also a seed, the seed of the soul. We all have the same seed at our core, the same spark of divinity – we are all part of the one eternal omnipresent Spirit. We are all part of the forest of humanity, an integral part of the forest of divinity.

When I live without 'conscious connection' to this seed I may experience an empty and limited existence. When I am conscious of this seed in myself and acknowledge this same seed exists in all of life, I may have a totally new and different experience.

Isn't it exciting, the wisdom we gain from nature? Imagine how our world would be if everyone acknowledged the seed of their soul. There is hope. Hope begins with a seed. A seed of thought planted in the fertile field of limitless mind. You pause in awe of this forest and say, "Ode to a tree, for all you have taught me."

You were not even aware that you were moving through the forest, and amazingly you find yourself on the edge of the lush field of limitless paths. The trail is wide... and you are not alone.

" Peace is an inner process before
it is an outer experience."

Bibliography

Embracing Our Selves – Hal Stone Ph.D. & Sidra
Winkelman Ph.D.
1989 New World Library, 58 Paul Drive, San Rafael, CA
94903
1985 Devorss & Co, Marina del Ray, CA

Healing Words - Dr. Larry Dossey
1993 HarperCollins Publishers – 10 E 53rd St, New York
10022

Women's Bodies Women's Wisdom - Dr. C. Northrop
1995, 1998, 2002 Random House Publishing Division of
Bantam Books-1540 Broadway, New York 10036

Healing with Whole Foods - Paul Pitchford
1993 North Atlantic Books-PO Box 12327 Berkley, CA 94701

Prescription for Dietary Wellness - Using Foods to Heal -
Drs. Phyllis & James Baulch
1992 Avery Publishing Group Inc-120 Old Broadway,
Garden City Park, New York 10040

Anatomy Coloring Workbook - I. Edward Alcamo, Ph.D
1997 Princeton Review Publishing-2315 Broadway, NY 10024

Spiritual Economics - Eric Butterworth
1989 Unity School of Christianity-Unity Village, MO 64065

The Prophet - Kahlil Gibran
1923, Borzoi Book Published by Alfred A. Knoff Inc. NY
1992, In Canada by Random House, Toronto

Waking the Tiger - Healing Trauma
1987 North Atlantic Books, PO Box 12317, Berkley CA 94712

Healing the Shame That Blinds You - John Bradshaw
1989 HCI Audio Books - Health Communication Inc. 3201S.W. 15th St. Deerfield Beach, FL 33442

Heartmath - Doc Lew Childre & Sara Paddison
1995 Planetary Publications-PO Box 66, Boulder Creek, CA 95066

Peaceful Conflict Resolution - Poster - Robert E. Vallett

You Can Heal Your Life - Louise L. Hay
1984 Hay House Inc. Santa Monica CA

Heal Your Body - Louise L. Hay
1982 Hay House Inc. PO Box 5100, Carlsbad, CA 92018-5100

The Four Agreements - Don Miguel Ruiz
1987 Amber Allen - PS Box 6657 San Rafael, CA 94903

Path of Transformation - Shakti Gawain
1993 Nataraj Publishing - PO Box 2627 Mill Valley, CA 94942

How to Change Your Life - Dr. Ernest Holmes
1982 Science of Mind Publications-3251 W. Sixth St. PO Box 75127, LA, CA 90075

Webster's II - New Riverside Edition
1984 Houghton Miffin Co. - 1 Beacon St. Boston MA 02108
A Berkley Book - Berkley Publishing Group-200 Madison NY 10016

Happiness is an Inside Job - John S. Powell
1989 Tabor Publishing - 1 DLM Park, Allen, Texas 75002

The New Possibilty Thinkers Bible
1996 Thomas Nelson Publishers - PO Box 14100, Nashville, Tennessee 37214-1000

Building Your Field of Dreams - Mary Manin Morrissey
1996 Bantam Books - Bantam Doubleday Dell Publishing Group, 1540 Broadway, New York, 10036

Bodymind - Ken Dychtwald 1977, 1986 Pantheon Books, New York.
Published by: Jeremy P. Tarcher Inc, 5858 wilshire blud. L.A.CA. 90036

Huna - Beginner's Guide - Enid Hoffman
1976 - Para Research Inc. 85 Eastern Ave, Gloucester, MA 01930